Of Course
I'm for Monogamy

I'm Also for
Everlasting Peace
and an End
to Taxes

Also by Marilyn vos Savant

*The Power of Logical Thinking: Easy Lessons in the Art of Reasoning
and Hard Facts About Its Absence in Our Lives*

*"I've Forgotten Everything I Learned in School!":
A Refresher Course to Help You Reclaim Your Education*

*The World's Most Famous Math Problem: The Proof of
Fermat's Last Theorem and Other Mathematical Mysteries*

Ask Marilyn

More Marilyn

Marilyn vos Savant

Of Course I'm for Monogamy

I'm Also for Everlasting Peace and an End to Taxes

St. Martin's Griffin
New York

OF COURSE I'M FOR MONOGAMY: I'M ALSO FOR
EVERLASTING PEACE AND AN END TO TAXES.

Design by Chris Welch

Library of Congress Cataloging-in-Publication Data

Vos Savant, Marilyn Mach.
Of course I'm for monogamy : I'm also for everlasting peace and an
end to taxes / Marilyn vos Savant.—1st ed.
p. cm.
ISBN 0-312-16951-5
1. Questions and answers. I. Title
AG195.V68   1996
031.02—dc20   96-19402
                                                           CIP

First St. Martin's Griffin Edition: October 1997

10   9   8   7   6   5   4   3   2   1

To Larry and Stephen
and all the Jelms of the world

Contents

Acknowledgments   x

Introduction   xi

1. On the Human Condition   1
   "Our light shoes scuff dark, but our dark shoes
   scuff light."

2. On Relationships   8
   "Of *course* I'm for monogamy. I'm also for everlasting
   peace and an end to taxes."

3. On Intelligence   16
   "Friends will move on and facts will be fleeting, but
   wisdom is a permanent condition."

4. On Laws and Morals   26
   "It's midnight. Do you know where *you* are?"

5. On Government   39
   "I can't think of any greater harm to humanity
   than the kind that's done by good people who
   embrace a bad cause."

6. On Economics   44

"Your earning power is far greater than your
saving power."

7. On Political Correctness   65

"You can't even call someone 'spineless' anymore;
you have to call him 'an invertebrate.'"

8. On Getting Ahead   75

"Being beaten is often a temporary condition; giving
up is what makes it permanent."

9. On Nature   82

"Even a wise old owl doesn't have the foggiest notion
that mating may produce little owlets, and he doesn't
give a hoot, either."

10. On Science   100

"If you put an air mattress and a water bed in the same
cool room, you'll sleep just fine on the air mattress, but
you'll have to heat the water bed."

11. On Thinking Analytically   113

"Think of mental exercise like physical exercise."

12. On Games, Gaming, and Gambling   131

"Mary, if I knew how to answer your question, we
wouldn't need lotteries anymore."

13. On Math Problems   143

"This chapter will keep you up half the night. . . ."

14. On Logic Puzzles   161

"... And this chapter will keep you up for the *other* half!"

15. On Mysticism   174

"We can all have opinions about flavors, colors, and sounds, but we shouldn't have opinions about the Tooth Fairy."

16. On the Arts   180

"This is art?"

17. On the Personal Side   186

"I practice what I preach. That's why I try *never* to preach."

18. On the Funniest Questions   196

Marilyn, how do they fit all that hot air into blow-dryers? Why don't they ever run out?

How to Send a Question to "Ask Marilyn"   211

About the Author   212

Acknowledgments

I gratefully acknowledge my dear friend and editor Sara Brzowsky, who has taught me the difference between meaning what I say and saying what I mean. She improves my work immeasurably.

Introduction

After finally getting to the bottom of a pile of mail over 250,000 letters deep, I think it's time for a juice-and-cookie break! Much to my mail carrier's dismay (and my delight), we've been heaping up this teetering stack for a decade now. (I guess the post office is right; I need a bigger mailbox.)

But not all the envelopes I receive contain questions from the readers whom I've come to know and love (although their contents are sometimes questionable, all right). The mail also contains home-baked goodies, lottery tickets, and marriage proposals, not to mention a recent request from an eighty-two-year-old widow for Bruce Willis's phone number. (Well, she *is* a widow, remember. But anyway, I wouldn't dream of giving out Bruce Willis's home phone number. I keep it for my *own* use.) So as much as I've tried to entertain and educate my readers, they've also entertained and educated *me*. (And without even trying.)

Here you'll find the most challenging, the funniest, the best, and the worse of it—what people all over the country like to think about, laugh about, and argue about every Sunday morning over blueberry pancakes or antacid tablets. Forging a long-term (monogamous, of *course*) relationship with 70 million Americans hasn't been easy, and I think a celebration is in order. But according to whoever decides these things, the gift for a ten-year anniversary is tin. *Tin?!* (What company's slogan is "Say it with foil"?) So I've decided to stick around for a while—for the eleventh anniversary, it's steel. For gifts, I'll get everything *including* the kitchen sink.

One

On the Human Condition

"Our light shoes scuff dark,
but our dark shoes scuff light."

Dear Marilyn:
   What is your own definition of "the human condition"?

                                    Robert Garelli, Jr.
                                    Chicopee, Massachusetts

Speaking for myself, I think "the human condition" describes that decades-long predicament of passion and pain in which we all find ourselves, born more alike than different, proceeding more different than alike, living together, and dying alone.

Dear Marilyn:
   Here's a philosophical question for you. I've had a personal disappointment, and everyone tells me that I'll feel better with time, but I'm not so sure. Do you think it's true that time heals all wounds?

                                    Bill Draper
                                    Brooksville, Florida

No, I don't. I think that time heals *many* wounds, but others will just get infected. So the wise person will take the trouble to keep that wound clean and covered for a while.

Dear Marilyn:
   Do you think it's true that "the squeaky wheel gets the most oil"?

                                    Mike Ditton
                                    Eugene, Oregon

Sometimes. But it's also the one that gets replaced first with a new wheel.

Dear Marilyn:
   One of my pet peeves is people who think one thing and say another. You don't do ever that, do you?

                                    Sharon Pelham
                                    Westboro, Massachusetts

Prepare to be peeved—yes, I do. But it's usually when the person to whom I'm talking would definitely prefer not to hear what I'm thinking.

Dear Marilyn:

We recently heard a definition of the word "humble" that goes like this: "You're never as big as you think you are, nor as small as you make yourself out to be." What do you think of this definition?

Joseph Collino
Delray Beach, Florida

Not much. It doesn't sound like a definition to me—it sounds like biting commentary about *false* modesty, instead. But if you don't mind commentary, here's a letter from a reader who inadvertently shows himself to be a model of humility for us all. "Dear Marilyn," he wrote. "I took an intelligence test as part of a program for a new position for which I was being considered, and the psychologist in charge was astounded. He said I was a genius! I started to laugh to myself. The problems on that test were so easy!" And then the reader added, "I lost all confidence in IQ tests after that." Now, that's *humble*!

Dear Marilyn:

What is the difference between loving yourself and vanity?

Doug Larsen
Council Bluffs, Iowa

When you love yourself, you forgive your imperfections. But when you're vain, you don't even know you have them.

Dear Marilyn:

What is your definition of maturity?

C. G. Basse
Evansville, Indiana

It's when you stop doing the things that you have to make excuses for, and when you stop making excuses for the things you have to do.

Dear Marilyn:

A few years ago, at age 41, an extraordinary thing occurred. I was walking alone, when suddenly, I came to myself! For the first time in my life, I knew I was here. Before that event, my life happened *to* me, but now I am the one acting upon life.

My sister says that I have always made my own choices. I say that before I woke up, I was unable to choose and therefore not responsible. Until this day, I do not understand exactly what happened. Did "childhood" end that day? And which of us do you think is correct?

Mrs. Claymore
Ohio

When we consider how many people there are in the world, we shouldn't be surprised that the period of "growing up" ranges from one extreme to another. Some of us never grow up at all, some take many years to do it, and some take only a few years. However, you're the first person I've ever heard of that grew up in only a few *minutes.*

But maturing is not the same as becoming responsible, and I don't agree with either you or your sister. I believe that as a person grows older, he or she becomes more and more responsible for himself or herself and should be judged accordingly, relative to the standards of the community. In general, the more serious our action, the more obviously wrong (or right) it is, and so the younger we can be held responsible for it.

That is, a normal six-year-old knows perfectly well that it is wrong to do physical harm to another, but he may not know that he shouldn't gather a basket of the strawberries in his neighbor's garden. I'd hold him responsible for the former but not for the latter.

Dear Marilyn:

How do you know when you're middle-aged?

Robert Rosenbloom
Port St. Lucie, Florida

You know you're middle-aged when you get up in the morning and hear the "snap, crackle, and pop" *before* you get to the breakfast table.

Dear Marilyn:

Do you think that it is best for a middle-aged person to live as though she doesn't have much time left, or to live as though she expects to see old age?

Ginny Boyd
Redlands, California

If I were you, I'd treat my loved ones as though I had only a few years left, and I'd treat my money as though I expected to live to a hundred.

Dear Marilyn:

Generally, how old is a person when others stop saying to him, "You have your whole life ahead of you"?

Connie Malevitsis
Seattle, Washington

They stop saying it when he's old enough to know better.

Dear Marilyn:

In order to become stronger mentally, one can read good books and engage in stimulating conversation. In order to develop physically, one can eat a well-balanced diet and exercise regularly. In order to grow spiritually, one can meditate on one's scriptures and pray. How does one become stronger emotionally?

James Boyd
Oceanside, California

You've hit upon one of my favorite private admonitions, and I'm pleased to have a chance to express it. I believe that one becomes stronger emotionally by having more experience and *by taking life less personally*. That is, if your employer criticizes your report, don't take it personally; instead, find out what was needed and fix it. If your girlfriend laughs at your tie, don't take it personally; find another tie or another girlfriend. When you get sick or robbed or jilted, you'll be less likely to waste your time and energy with thoughts of "Why *me*?" And above all, if the newspapers ever celebrate your very existence on this planet, don't take it personally. Remember, these are the same folks whom you call fools when they find fault with you.

✖

Dear Marilyn:
    Whom does an atheist fear?

                                            Julian Hammer
                                            Carteret, New Jersey

An atheist fears himself.

✖

Dear Marilyn:
    I saw a television program a few years ago that highlighted the life of a certain world-famous person prior to his becoming famous. At one point in his life, he was a philosophy professor, and during that part of the program, he was quoted as saying, "A true realist demands the impossible." After I thought about this statement for a while, it made sense. My question to you is, what would a true *idealist* demand?

                                            Martin J. Ibbott
                                            Baltimore, Maryland

A true idealist demands the impractical.

✖

Dear Marilyn:
    What quality do you feel is the most important for a human being to possess? I tend to think love and compassion and perseverance are the most important qualities we need in order to live happy, successful lives.

                                            Marie Skertic
                                            Delran, New Jersey

I'd say it's "honor." Although happiness and success seem to be good goals, the living of a truly honorable life makes the attainment of goals unnecessary.

✖

Dear Marilyn:
    Children and adults alike admire celebrities such as television, movie, sports, and rock stars because they're part of a fantasy world to

which people enjoy escaping. But we take them on as heroes based only on their public images. Celebrities are just regular people like everyone else, and we know nothing about their morals, values, or character. Should people keep the positive images they have of celebrities, or should they risk disillusionment by learning what they really are?

N. Michaels
Anaheim, California

I think it's fine to have positive images of celebrities *and* fine to be disillusioned by anything we might learn about them. After all, that's how we treat our friends and neighbors, and celebrities are no different from the rest of us as far as personal qualities are concerned. But I believe we should never take on an ordinary celebrity as a *hero*. Instead, I'd reserve the title of *"hero"* for the men and women of superior courage and nobility of purpose who voluntarily take great personal risks (whether private or professional) for praiseworthy public causes (whether involving one person or many), achieving truly deserved stature as a result.

Dear Marilyn:
 Did prehistoric man have "spare" time?

Matt Lusk
Lexington, Virginia

Yes. Otherwise, there wouldn't be so many of us now.

Dear Marilyn:
 I assume you've heard the saying, "You're damned if you do, and you're damned if you don't." I think it's the story of my life. Is this a common problem, or is it just me?

Joey Presser
Tupelo, Mississippi

It's the same with all of us. Our light shoes scuff dark, but our dark shoes scuff light.

Two

On Relationships

"Of <u>course</u> I'm for monogamy.
I'm also for everlasting peace
and an end to taxes."

Dear Marilyn:

A special gentleman and I recently had a disagreement that ended our relationship. The argument was about monogamy, and I, being pro-monogamy, concluded by saying, "We aren't animals!" He, arguing *against* monogamy, said that we *are* animals and that the desire for multiple partners is natural and that he sees nothing wrong with it. Is there anything unique to the human animal that encourages monogamy that is not present in other animals? And are *you* for monogamy?

Anonymous
Pacific Grove, California

Well, as for your first question, paternity suits seem to help! And of *course* I'm for monogamy. I'm also for everlasting peace and an end to taxes.

Dear Marilyn:

Do you know of any logical reason why there are plenty of decent guys who can't find someone to marry, but there are plenty of not-so-decent guys who manage to get married time after time?

Bill Bangert
Douglas, Georgia

Some men are loveable, but not likeable; some men are likeable, but not loveable. The first kind have trouble getting a wife; the second kind have trouble *keeping* her.

Dear Marilyn:

My boyfriend and I are taking the same philosophy course, and we've gotten into some heated discussions about morals and ethics. What irritates me is that he lectures me as though his interpretation is always the correct one. He sounds just like his father, who lectures his mother the same way. I don't know how she's been able to stand it all these years. But other than that, he's Mr. Right. What should I do?

B.B.
Fresno, California

You haven't found Mr. Right; you've found Mr. Righteous. If I were you, I'd stand up to the challenge and force him to defend his premises or vacate them. And be sure to take plenty of courses together over the next few years. It'll help to prepare both of you for what lies ahead in the next few *decades*.

Dear Marilyn:

My husband has a heart of gold, but he says that if he isn't happy, then no one else in this family is going to be happy, and he's been proven right time and time again. What do *you* think about it?

Anonymous
Montgomery, Alabama

I don't think your husband has a heart of gold; I think he has a heart of *brass*.

Dear Marilyn:

I know you don't give personal advice, but I could use a totally cool opinion on a matter important to me. I'm going with a nice guy whose family is involved, to put it mildly, in some dangerous activities, if you know what I mean. My mother doesn't want me to ever consider marrying him even though she likes him okay, but my friends all say that he should be judged on himself alone, not on his relatives too. What do *you* think?

Anonymous
Brooklyn, New York

I think we make more mistakes by judging people out of context than we do by taking the whole situation into consideration. And in this case, his relatives may not stay in the background! In sum, marriage is difficult enough without having outlaws for in-laws. If I were you, I'd end the relationship, and if you find yourself without a date this weekend as a result, try staying at home with a big bowlful of popcorn and an old *Godfather* videotape. Do some nice gal a favor whose *own* family is involved in those activities, and let *her* have him. At least she'll know what to expect.

Dear Marilyn:
    What is the best cure for unrequited love?

                                        Heather Aston
                                        New Brunswick, New Jersey

Well, lunch with the ex-wife or ex-husband has certainly dampened a
lot of torches.

Dear Marilyn:
    Some psychologists say that humans are the only animals that can
become totally reliant on their mates. Is this true?

                                        Joe Shurtz
                                        Kansas City, Kansas

Ever heard of the angler fish? In some types, the male buries his teeth
into the female and then proceeds to hang on for dear life. His mouth
gradually fuses there, and not only do his eyes glaze over, even the rest
of his body quits working. Eventually, he just becomes a big, funny-
looking blob capable of not much more than reproduction. Now, that's
dependency! (Female readers should try to resist the temptation to write
and tell me this sounds exactly like their husbands.)

Dear Marilyn:
    If real violence is banned on television, why not also censor sitcoms
that show perfect, unrealistic families living in a world untouched by
death, divorce, or even bad language? Compared to watching violence,
isn't it just as dangerous for impressionable children to see these
picture-book households and form lasting, inaccurate ideas about
family life?

                                        Bennett Haselton
                                        Copenhagen, Denmark

Why stop there, Bennett? Why not show every misfortune and vice
known to humankind? In other words, why should we broadcast the

bad side of realism instead of the good side? As far as impressionable children are concerned, I cast my vote for the benefit of a good example.

Dear Marilyn:

A friend and I were discussing families, and we decided that no family is normal. We also decided that "normal" is a word made up by psychiatrists to make us all feel neurotic and promote business! What is "normal," and who decided this?

Deanna Jardon
San Francisco, California

The word actually has quite a few very different meanings, depending on the scientific discipline. (For example, in chemistry, "normal" can be the designation for a hydrocarbon that has a straight chain of carbon atoms.) But the "normal" to which you refer has two definitions that have become inappropriately intermingled lately. One definition is "typical"; the other definition is "free from emotional disorder." So all of us, as a society, define what is a "typical" family just by being ourselves; the psychiatrists are the ones who define who is "free from emotional disorder," which is a diagnosis of elimination. That is, people with emotional disorders are relatively obvious; the rest of us are "normal."

Typical families produce both children who are just fine and children who are a pain in the neck. And non-typical families produce children who are just fine and children who are a pain in the neck. The problem arises when we see a troubled child and then go back and label his or her *family* "dysfunctional." Because so many family types produce so many fine *and* not-so-fine kids, this way of thinking labels *all* families dysfunctional, leading to the sort of comment you made.

Some of us do everything wrong, and the kids turn out okay. Others of us do somersaults for the kids, and they *still* turn out troublesome. And then someone comes along and says the fact that we turned somersaults is the *reason* they turned out troublesome!

Dear Marilyn:

Did your parents say the words, "I love you," while you were growing up and in later years? Many children and adults wish their parents had said, "I love you," at least once while the parents were still living. They wanted and needed to hear those three important words.

Vickie Eddy
Olean, New York

No, my parents didn't do that, but it was totally unnecessary. Why, I didn't have to be told that my mother and father loved me any more than I had to be told that the sun comes up every morning. It was *obvious*!

Dear Marilyn:
How do you feel about women donating their time as Girl Scout leaders?

Nancy Walty
Encinitas, California

I think it's an invaluable experience, not just for the youngsters involved, but also for the women themselves. In fact, I'd recommend it to all mothers with daughters, whether the mother works outside the home or not, and preferably for at least one year with the daughter in the same troop. This volunteer work is a good deed for the community as a whole—scouting is obviously an enriching experience—but there are more personal benefits as well. The daughter gets to see how dozens of other youngsters—from close friends to distant acquaintances—relate to her mother as a person, and the mother gets to see how those same youngsters relate to her daughter. I was a Girl Scout leader myself, and during one year, I learned as much about my daughter from the other kids as I learned from my daughter herself.

Dear Marilyn:
What is your opinion on this philosophical question? Does the love between two people (like a mother and daughter who are very close) "die" when one of them dies? I ask this very seriously, and I don't mean the memory of the love—I mean the love itself.

W. T. G.
Largo, Florida

I think that love becomes immortalized upon the death of one of the people involved, although the position of importance it occupies in our lives will fade with time. There's some scientific evidence of this. Psychiatrists and psychologists have found that the death of a parent, for example, does not resolve the problem that a son or daughter may have had with that parent. Instead, the relationship becomes "frozen" because no further personal interaction is possible. So I'd say that regardless of whether we think about it often or not, love lives on and on.

Dear Marilyn:

I know you're not an advice columnist, but I need some personal advice of a more philosophical kind, so I'm writing to you anyway. I have two relatives who are getting very old and can't live much longer, and I know my mother will want me to go to their funerals when the time comes. I still live in my old hometown, so that isn't a problem. The trouble is that I think funerals are for the living, not for the people who've died. What do you think about it? Should I go?

Jack Marlebitz
Corvallis, Oregon

Go. I agree that funerals are for the living, and that includes *you*. Nobody ever regrets attending a funeral or a wedding. (Unless the wedding was your own, that is.)

Dear Marilyn:

I'm a rector in our church, and in my sixty-five years on this earth, I've never heard a really truthful eulogy. My question to you is, why don't they tell the truth about him or her? If he was a lousy person, why not just say so?

Suelo Semana
Waimea, Hawaii

Eulogies aren't intended to be truthful, and even by its very definition, a eulogy is "a laudatory speech." But if you really think telling the truth is a better idea, why not write that provision into your will? That is, issue a request for everyone attending your funeral to please get up and say a few painfully honest words about you, like, "Well, Suelo was a pretty decent guy most of the time, but you just wouldn't believe what he did one Saturday night back in 1948. It all started when—" By the end of this, people may have begun to take back their flowers and leave, but that's the price you pay for honesty!

Dear Marilyn:

I know you don't answer etiquette questions, but I'm hoping you'll apply your powers of reasoning to this one. I've read that it's a waste to send flowers to a funeral and that sending a check to a charity in the name of the deceased makes much more sense. My best friend agrees, but something just doesn't feel right to me about it. What do *you* say?

Linda Palmer
Provo, Utah

Your friend isn't thinking straight. Of all things to drop from our lives, why in the world should we target flowers? Why are flowers at funerals more wasteful than candy on Mother's Day or ties on Father's Day? (And don't tell me it's because the deceased doesn't see the flowers; he doesn't see the donation, either. The flowers are there for the grieving.) It makes far more sense to drop something harmful from our lives—like trashy books or violent movies or ugly entertainment—and donate *that* money to charity, instead.

Dear Marilyn:

Most of us clutter up our small houses with things that are of no value, such as worn-out shoes or old pencils. I always think I'm going to use them, but I never do, and when we move, we take these things with us, only to store them again. How can you tell the difference between what's of sentimental value and what's just junk?

Mary G.
St. Petersburg, Florida

I believe *positive* sentiments are the only ones worth keeping over the years. If you don't actually use an item, you should keep it only if it gives you pleasure to see it; otherwise, give it away or junk it. (Husbands and wives are an exception, Mary.)

Three

On Intelligence

"Friends will move on and facts
will be fleeting, but wisdom
is a permanent condition."

Dear Marilyn:

At the age of seventy-seven, aware of my mortality, I've been sorting papers, and until today, I wasn't aware that my IQ score had been recorded. In contrast to yours, I discovered papers from the army that list mine as a moronic 100! After serving in World War II, I finished my education, earning a bachelor's degree, a master's degree, and other professional degrees. If I were tested now, would my education have changed my IQ? I'm glad I pursued my studies without knowing I was a nincompoop!

Lee Friedman
Flushing, New York

Supposedly, IQ measures cognitive ability and has little to do with education, but intelligence-testing is controversial. So I hope you won't mind if I voice one of my strongest feelings about the subject. (Your experience in life is a perfect example—so is the negative way you appraised your score.)

I want to suggest a major change in the way we label our intelligence. Normal vision is 20/20 (measured in feet). If your vision is 20/20, you can see what normal eyes can see. We call this "perfect" vision, and we're delighted if we have it. Normal intelligence is 100 (measured by IQ). If your IQ is 100, you are as intelligence as a normal person. *Let's begin to call this "perfect" intelligence.* It's about time!

Dear Marilyn:

Why does it seem that extremely intelligent people exhibit an air of humility while some people who are just plain intelligent are really hard to live with?

John Smalling
Alcoa, Tennessee

The brightest people I know answer questions less quickly, add more restrictions to their replies, and say, "I'm not sure," more often than others. However, this is not because they're more modest. Instead, it's often because they're intelligent enough to comprehend the vast expanse of human understanding and how little of it any one person can master in a lifetime.

Dear Marilyn:

I told my wife, who disagrees, that an individual can be educated beyond his or her level of competence. I'd appreciate your point of view.

John Drewes
Birmingham, Alabama

I could hardly agree with you more. I've personally met many of these individuals, and they're clearly responsible for much of the stagnation and outright bad judgment in their fields. However, because they're well educated, they're assumed by outsiders to be highly qualified. (Insiders know better.) In the past, these people were mainly scattered (less harmfully) throughout the sciences, but lately, they've begun turning up in government, and that's even worse. Science projects that don't work are usually far less harmful than political and social experiments, especially on a federal scale.

Dear Marilyn:

Since an IQ test consists primarily of English and math, do you feel that it accurately measures a person's intelligence?

Henry Philippeaux
Wheatley Heights, New York

You're referring to the multiple-choice, group-administered intelligence tests that are easy to score and inexpensive to conduct. But the best IQ tests cover a far broader range of abilities and never consist of multiple-choice answers; they're always administered by a trained clinician with a single individual testee and take several hours to conduct. (I've taken them myself.) However, this makes them expensive and relatively seldom used, which is why so many of us are unaware of their existence. I, too, hold the "mass" tests in relatively low regard, but I wouldn't spend precious education funds on the better ones, which I don't hold in such high regard, either.

Dear Marilyn:

Can you tell us, generally speaking, which sex is smarter—male or female? Is there any valid way to find out, such as an IQ test?

Jonathan Lang
Vista, California

You'll be interested to know that since the turn of the century (when IQ tests were first established)—despite the deeply pervasive belief that women were not as intelligent as men and despite the extremely strong discouragement of women from developing their intellectual potential—both males and females have continued to score similarly on IQ tests. (By the way, I personally don't believe that IQ tests are adequate measures of intelligence, but at present, they're the only yardsticks around.)

Dear Marilyn:

Why do people assume that certain scientists are smarter than other people? We hear expressions like, "It doesn't take a rocket scientist to realize that . . ." (It used to be, "It doesn't take a nuclear physicist . . .") How come I've never heard anyone say, "It doesn't take a journalism teacher [my profession] to realize that. . . ." However, in Sunday school recently, I did hear someone say, "It doesn't take a vos Savant to realize that . . ."

> Art Trujillo
> Las Vegas, New Mexico

Well, we're making progress, aren't we?! I believe the reason people assume that certain scientists are brighter is that the terminology used in those certain sciences is majestic (like galaxies), unfamiliar (like superstring theory), and downright weird (like gauge bosons and fermions and gravitons). Because of this overarching obscurity, outsiders don't know how to judge whether insiders are right, wrong, average, or just plain nuts—but they certainly *sound* impressive. And indeed they may be.

But because relatively few people are scientists and because many people in the overall population are unusually bright, my educated guess is that there are far more exceptionally intelligent people outside the sciences than inside them. And thank goodness for that. Maybe it's time to stop channeling bright people into positions behind microscopes and start channeling them into positions behind microphones instead. Posts of communication and leadership are clearly much more important—especially in Washington, D.C. Still, I predict the day will *never* come when we say, "It doesn't take a politician to realize that . . ."

Dear Marilyn:

Do you believe in the notion that man cannot and never will "invent," he merely "discovers"? If we merely discover, why is there so much attention and money paid to the U.S. Patent Office to protect these so-called inventions?

C. LeMond
San Diego, California

No, I don't believe that, and it sounds like sour grapes to me. Surely no one thinks that William Shakespeare merely "discovered" *Romeo and Juliet* among all the words available to him or that a pharmaceutical company spends a hundred million dollars and employs fifty people for ten years to merely "discover" a new drug for heart disease among all the elements known to mankind.

Dear Marilyn:

Let's say we compare an average group of eighteen-year-olds and an average group of sixty-five-year-olds. Both groups take the same course taught by the same instructor in a field that is foreign to them all. Do you think that the sixty-five-year-olds will absorb and retain as much knowledge as the eighteen-year-olds? Your answer may prevent a domestic disaster, as my wife and I have been sharply divided for years on this subject.

Joseph Angelo
Spring Hill, Florida

Because it appears that you want to isolate the factor of age, let's also say that the sixty-five-year-olds have been in school full-time for the last twelve straight years (like the eighteen-year-olds have been) and that they are equally as healthy, idealistic about what the future holds for them, willing to take instruction from people aged twenty-five to sixty-five, and unencumbered by personal and professional responsibilities (such as caring for others and/or making a living). In other words, all relevant considerations—these and many more—should be both equal and up-to-date, including computer skills.

Given those conditions (which are absent in real life), I think the sixty-five-year-olds and eighteen-year-olds might well perform closer to the same than we might otherwise assume. Due to the mature folks' vast experience in life, I would expect them to be ahead in subjects like psychology, social studies, political science, literature, and philosophy. And because the younger generation's natural curiosity can give them greater tolerance for the more tedious detail of the sciences, I would expect them to be likewise ahead in subjects like biology and physics and mathematics.

In short, I think much of the apparent difference in brainpower between the two groups may be due to circumstances other than biological ones, and I'd sure like to see more research done in this area. The reverse has been taken for granted for too long already.

Dear Marilyn:

Some friends and I have a dispute over the intelligence of different species. I say that humans are definitely the most intelligent creatures ever to walk the earth. They all disagree, saying that while humans are probably the most intelligent now, we don't know if there were superior creatures long before us that once ruled the world. Who's right?

Kamilah Turner
Memphis, Tennessee

I think you are. None of us can verify everything firsthand, and if we insisted on doing so, it would cripple the progress of civilization. (Do your friends believe that men landed on the Moon? If so, how do they *know*? Do they believe in the Easter Bunny? If not, how do they *know*?) While we have no absolute proof that there were no brighter creatures before us, the evidence leading to that conclusion is abundant. Moreover, we have no evidence at all to the contrary.

Dear Marilyn:

I have a nine-year-old daughter who is very smart—on the honor roll, in advanced classes, etc. But sometimes she says or does really stupid things. It seems as if she has no common sense. And I don't think it's the age because I know some adults with college educations and white-collar jobs who are the same way. How do you teach people, especially children, to use "common sense"?

J.C.
New Brunswick, New Jersey

Let me just relate my own experience around people of all sorts of intelligence. Whether they're bright or not, the ones who seem to have "no common sense" are often those who are somehow sheltered from the outside world, and this often starts in childhood. Common sense comes from experience, and kids need to fail as well as succeed in order to learn it. It's difficult to develop common sense when you spend a lot of time in your room where nothing much happens.

Dear Marilyn:

If you make a decision that causes embarrassment in front of many people, how do you recover? For example, an umpire makes a wrong call that even he later realizes was wrong.

Bob Mendoza
Fresno, California

You can recover only by demonstrating that you know the correct decision, so as soon as you discover your error, announce it to those same people. This will restore the confidence of those who knew you were wrong, and it will endear you to those who didn't.

Dear Marilyn:

My husband and I have a "black, white, and gray" problem. He believes that a person should never make a black-and-white statement and insists that you should always leave an "out" for yourself by using phrases like "I think." When I am in conversation with another person, he insists that I always leave a gray area, and he has instilled this belief into our children. However, I am a very positive thinker and was taught by my own father to be able to prove my statements. What do *you* think about this?

Glenis Comer
Fresno, California

Your husband's beliefs are inherently self-contradictory. (That was a black-and-white statement.) That is, when he insists that you *always* leave a gray area, he makes a black-and-white statement himself. If he left a gray area, he'd have to say that sometimes people should make black-and-white statements and sometimes they should leave gray areas! (But let's give him credit for only "believing" this and not stating it as a fact!)

Dear Marilyn:

I have a clay statue on my mantelpiece. A friend of mine, who is a philosophy student, has argued that it is really not one thing, but two. The first thing is a statue which can be gravely harmed by squeezing. The second is a lump of clay which cannot be harmed no matter how much you squeeze it. It seems to me that there is really only one thing on my mantelpiece, but I don't know how to answer him. Can you help me?

Eric Schwitzgebel
Berkeley, California

Ask your friend how many things *he* is. Let's say that first, he's a human being who can be gravely harmed by squeezing him too hard, and second, he's just a big sackful of chemicals (mainly ordinary water) that cannot be harmed even if flattened by a steamroller. But why stop there? Maybe third, he's a young man who *likes* to be squeezed, especially by an attractive member of the opposite sex. And fourth, he could be a philosophy student whose primary source of weekend entertainment is provoking existential crises in people who *aren't* philosophy students. In other words, why stop at two things on your mantelpiece? Why not go on forever? Where does it all end? (Good heavens. I've begun to sound like a philosophy student!)

Dear Marilyn:

How does a person know if he should "speak his mind"?

Joe Froeward
Las Vegas, Nevada

Your state of mind is what's important; everything else is secondary. That is, if your mind is open, it's all right for your mouth to be open. But if your mind is closed, your mouth should be likewise.

Dear Marilyn:
What's the difference between a reason and an excuse?

                                          Herb Stalter
                                          Columbus, Ohio

A "reason" is a persuasive basis for an action; an "excuse" is a basis that is *not* persuasive. That is, the concept is very subjective if you make decisions based on your emotions. But to the hard-hearted, too many reasons are believed to be excuses; and to the soft-hearted, too many excuses are believed to be reasons. The concept becomes more objective only if you make decisions based on your thoughts, which I consider best. After all, emotional education isn't taught in school, and life's lessons are too often too late.

Dear Marilyn:
Is there a difference between "knowing" something and simply "remembering" it? For example, do you *know* that two and two are four, or do you just remember the multiplication table?

                                          Helene Boyles
                                          San Diego, California

I believe that much of "knowledge" is indeed merely "memory," and this is why so many misconceptions persist for such a long time in the human population. For example, science is rife with error, but because so many people are so thoroughly schooled in the common misconceptions, only the most brilliantly skeptical of them will ever discover a mistake. And even then, it will likely be denied for generations to come. If the error has cultural importance, too, generations stretch into centuries.

Dear Marilyn:
Would you agree that if we could remember just half of what we've already read, we'd all be geniuses?

                                          Anonymous
                                          New Orleans, Louisiana

Nope. Consider the best possible reference library, containing all the important knowledge in the world. Would it be a genius? No. Remembering information is nowhere near as important as understanding it. (But we'd all make dandy game-show contestants, wouldn't we?)

Dear Marilyn:

The following question was asked by my young nephew, and I could not answer it with real conviction. If one learns factual information but later forgets the facts, was there any gain in value? I recognize that one needs only a general understanding of, for example, economics, in order to understand the free-market system. In this case, forgetting various specific facts does not negate the underlying learned principles. But is there any value to learning and forgetting more esoteric subjects, such as Greek mythology or even books of fiction?

Gordon Williams
Alpharetta, Georgia

Once the self-centered innocence of childhood is lost, it can never return, and so, I believe, it is the case with later learning, too. Fortunately (or not, in some cases!), normal people don't completely forget much of anything. Just as every good friend we make (whether accomplished or not) increases our social sophistication, every good book we read (whether fact or fiction) increases our intellectual understanding. In short, friends will move on and facts will be fleeting, but wisdom is a permanent condition.

Four

On Laws and Morals

"It's midnight. Do you know
where you are?"

Dear Marilyn:

In his great "I Have a Dream" speech, Martin Luther King, Jr., looked forward to a time when each person would be judged only by the "content of our characters." How would you propose that we do that? What would be your guidelines?

> Mary Berger
> Oakmont, Pennsylvania

The Ten Commandments are of utmost importance in the moral and ethical systems of Christianity, Islam, and Judaism. Five of them are religious in scope. How about using the five most secular commandments as a basis for the judgment of character? As they stand, they serve as warnings. But turned around and made positive, they can also serve as goals.

I. Heal those who have been harmed.
   (From "You shall not kill.")
II. Love all those who love you.
   (From "You shall not commit adultery.")
III. Give more to the world than you take.
   (From "You shall not steal.")
IV. Respect the dignity of truth.
   (From "You shall not bear false witness . . .")
V. Content yourself with the necessities.
   (From "You shall not covet your neighbor's . . .")

No one who lives by these guidelines need fear judgment.

Dear Marilyn:

Do you have a solution to the following dilemma?

An old man was taking a small boy on a trip, and the man hoisted the boy onto a donkey while he led the animal afoot. Soon they came upon another old man who chided the boy for showing no respect to his elders, so the boy alit from the donkey and the man climbed aboard. Then they came upon a young woman who chided the man for riding while the child walked, so the man hoisted the boy up alongside him. Then they came upon a woman who derided them both for placing such a burden upon a poor animal, so they both got off and walked alongside the donkey. And then they came upon a philosopher who shook his head in dismay that anyone could be so stupid as to walk when they had a donkey to ride.

What are we to do? Or do we just live life according to the adage, "You can't please everyone all the time"?

Julius Robichaux
Raceland, Louisiana

This scenario is a fine example of the meaning of the word "judgmental," which describes the behavior of all those people—the philosopher included—who formed moral opinions without taking the trouble to study the matter. So, what are we to do? We study the matter ourselves, we do the right thing, and we adhere to our principles despite the inevitable criticism we'll face along the way. And that old man, who behaved like a bad politician, was no better than his critics and perhaps worse than all of them put together. At least they were consistent.

❌

Dear Marilyn:

What is virtue? This is the question Socrates posed, and the primary question that my Western Civilizations class is attempting to answer. In reading various literary works, several interpretations of virtue have been discovered. Sophocles considered virtue to be obedience to the gods. St. Augustine regarded virtue as rejecting the temptations of the flesh. Enlightenment thinkers such as Voltaire believed virtue to be reason. What is your own definition or interpretation?

Linus Chen
Sudbury, Massachusetts

Personally, I find human virtue in the active quest for justice in this world. This would include rewarding goodness wherever it exists, paying no special attention to most things, and punishing truly harmful behavior. It would not include efforts to make all people equal regardless of their individual merits, which I find to be the ultimate human injustice.

For example, I find virtue in healing the sick. But if I were apportioning donor organs that are in short supply, I would bypass the chronic alcoholic who has destroyed her liver and instead give the next precious liver transplant to the patient who did little or nothing to bring about his condition.

I also find virtue in helping the poor. But if I were donating the funds, I would give financial aid to a woman who has been flooded out of her home and not to the habitual drug user who has been thrown out of the house because he is intolerable to have around.

This is not to say that I would be unwilling to help these categories of troubled people in other ways; in fact, I think that would be wise in many ways and would benefit both the individuals in particular and society as a whole. To illustrate, consider the public school system. It's clearly wise to have one, but I don't consider it a *virtue,* which is a different concept entirely.

As an opposite example, I do *not* find virtue in providing the best possible legal defense to people who have undoubtedly broken the law. If I were an attorney, I would not accept a client I believed to be guilty of an offense against society.

I also do not find virtue in providing a forum for free speech that is repugnant to both human sense and sensibility. If I owned a newspaper, I would not publish material that I believed to be in breach of all human ethical systems.

Of course, there are gray areas, but that's normal. Plenty of good goals require careful thought, foresight, and the exercise of courage. I do agree that virtue is its own reward—but this definition reverberates far beyond ourselves. Nothing brings more peace of mind to more people than justice does.

Dear Marilyn:
What's the one lesson in life that everyone should learn before he or she dies?

Eli Young
East Orange, New Jersey

It's good to be right, but it's right to be good.

Dear Marilyn:

Why do you think lawyers, as a group, have such a universal reputation for dishonesty? Could it be because the group has a disproportionate number of dishonest members?

Paige Andre-Hudson
De Funiak Springs, Florida

I've laughed at "lawyer" jokes myself, but I don't find evidence that attorneys are any less honest than the members of other occupational groups. Maybe one of the reasons they've developed that reputation is that their professional ethics require them to go to extreme lengths to defend even the most reprehensible characters in society, and this behavior has received broad exposure since the advent of television in the courtroom. (Note that we never denounce lawyers who defend the best of us.) Even in less sensational appearances, we routinely see attorneys trying to cast *each other* as liars, opportunists, and worse. But because it's part of the standard operating procedure, it doesn't tell us much about them as individuals. So if we're going to level ethical criticism and press for change, it makes more sense to target the principles of the legal profession itself, not the conduct of its members.

Dear Marilyn:

Why should a jury decision be unanimous for conviction?

John Stoner
Allentown, Pennsylvania

The Sixth Amendment to the U.S. Constitution provides the right to a jury trial in criminal cases, but there is no constitutional requirement that a jury be composed of twelve members or that its verdict be unanimous. The states make those decisions. So because the accused is presumed to be innocent until proven guilty and because it's so difficult to get that many people to agree on anything, a jury trial virtually ensures that no innocent person will be convicted. Unfortunately, it also ensures that most guilty people will not be convicted unless the evidence is so obvious that it convinces even the most foolish juror of the twelve. This is one of the reasons so many guilty defendants want jury trials. Opponents call the jury trial an amateurish ritual that has long outlived its usefulness, and my own experience as a juror on a murder trial was a sobering one. Perhaps the O. J. Simpson trial, regardless of the outcome, will serve as a catalyst for change.

First is the issue of competence. It is clear that a judge has the training, experience, and mental capacity to understand the case better than a group of ordinary citizens whose names literally have been drawn at random.

Second is the issue of understanding of the law. American political tradition is based in the rule of law and has always been set against rule by men. Yet juries can simply disregard the law, whether on purpose or by lack of understanding.

Third is the issue of cost and delay. Juries are very expensive and contribute heavily to the seemingly endless delays rampant in the judicial system. It takes far more time to present a case to them than to a judge.

The United States is increasingly alone on the floor as the rest of the world abandons the jury system it never embraced. Because so many civil-law countries have virtually eliminated it, more than 90 percent of all jury trials are now held in America. Despite that, I never thought I would find myself standing in front of eleven other people in a jury room to tell them my thoughts about what may have happened in an anonymous New York apartment on one particular night.

The charge was murder in the second degree and rape in the first degree. The judge said this was a simple case, and the trial commenced. We were shown three graphic crime scene photos, called People's Exhibit No. 1, followed by People's Exhibits Nos. 2 and 3—a knife and a pillowcase. The judge was intelligent and careful; the jury was a pack of wild cards. Not only was this sort of case foreign to most of us, we were not allowed to ask questions.

As the trial continued, we learned that fiber tests were inconclusive, as were hair tests and blood tests. *Nothing* was conclusive, including the medical reports. And to make matters worse, most of the witnesses— the dead woman's friends and other prostitutes—appeared to be lying. At the end, the judge charged us to reach a verdict. If all twelve could not agree on a "guilty" or "not guilty" verdict, a "hung" jury would result, and the trial would be repeated with a new jury.

Deliberations began, and we took turns speaking. A number of jurors were leaning toward conviction on both counts, but they weren't certain. The defendant may have committed the crimes, we all knew, but there was simply no physical evidence whatsoever—not a fiber, not a hair, not a single drop of blood. Should he be convicted anyway? The last to speak, I said that even if there had been a person among this group who had claimed to be an eyewitness, I would be hard pressed to vote "guilty" in the absence of *any* evidence.

The first vote on the rape charge was eleven for acquittal and one for conviction. After discussion, the second vote was unanimous for acquittal. More discussion followed, and by the end of the afternoon, the vote on the murder charge was unanimous for acquittal, too. When the defendant heard the "not guilty" verdict, tears streamed down his cheeks. We were back in the jury room to pick up our belongings when the court clerk suddenly burst through the door and gestured "thumbs up" with a big smile. "Great verdict!" she said. The jurors were taken aback. Unlike us, she seemed so certain.

A jubilant court police officer then arrived. "Thank heaven," she said. "I was so afraid for that poor guy. You did the right thing, and now an innocent man is going to go free!" This time the jurors appeared stunned. We were all keenly aware of how easily it could have gone the other way. Then the judge himself sent word that he was very pleased with our verdict. The jurors nearly stopped talking entirely. One said he felt silly.

How safe would we feel as a country if the procedure were to convene a random selection of citizens to make up the Supreme Court each time a case is to be decided upon? Do you think you'd feel safe with a jury? Maybe you'd better think again.

Dear Marilyn:

Until reading your column about juries in this country, we had never questioned our judicial system. Your comments opened our eyes. In answer to your question, "What Do You Think? Should we: (1) Leave the jury system as it is? or (2) Have juries composed of six judges, with decisions to be reached by supermajority vote—at least five votes out of six?" We vote for No. 2.

Ed and Jo Reynolds
San Diego, California

My father was a big fan of yours. He was killed while resisting a robbery. There were six eyewitnesses and an overwhelming amount of evidence against the defendant. A jury trial ended without a verdict because one juror stated that even though she thought he was guilty, she didn't want his conviction on her conscience. The judge was appalled. After the trial, I was surprised to discover that not all states require a unanimous verdict. And now you state that most civil-law countries have eliminated jury trials and that the U.S. alone now holds 90 percent of all jury trials! I vote for No. 2.

D.W.
Sacramento, California

Our system is a disgrace to American jurisprudence, a throwback to the time when it was meant to keep the lords from judging the serfs unfettered. No. 2.

Dan Raveed, Ph.D.
Indianapolis, Indiana

The courtrooms are filled with lawyers who are more interested in influencing the jurors than upholding the law. The O.J. trial is an embarrassment to our country. No. 2.

Jeanette Eckard
Pasco, Washington

The Simpson murder trial should be the last straw. A panel of judges would have put an end to his case in a matter of weeks. No. 2.

Melinda Coniff
Indianapolis, Indiana

First the Menendez case and now the O. J. Simpson trial. I am totally outraged and want change *now*. No. 2.

Lillian Papuzza
West Palm Beach, Florida

Perhaps someone with leadership ability can show the voters how to change the system. Please don't let this issue drop. No. 2.

Jack Peterson
St. Petersburg, Florida

You really hit a nerve with your column about the jury system. How can we bring such change about? No. 2.

Marvin Revell
Sun City, California

Your replies may surprise many people, especially those in high public office. Of the more than 1,300 readers who responded to my informal opinion survey, about 4 out of 5 (79.8 percent) would like to scrap the jury system entirely.

(A small number of them would replace it with professional jurors instead of judges. This is similar to a panel of judges, except that the professional jurors would be free to vote in accord with their consciences when they didn't like the law, much as citizen jurors do now. This can be viewed as a way to keep the government from engaging in oppression or persecution. However, we could easily empower judges to do the same.)

Only 1 out of 5 (20.2 percent) would like to leave the jury system much as it is. (Some of them dislike requirements of unanimity; many cited fear of the government.) However, it should be noted that a significant number of responses came from the members of a single advocacy group. Here are comments from readers who apparently wrote on their own initiative.

Dear Marilyn:

As the president of a national trial-lawyer association, I found your comments disquieting. Quite often a jury trial is not as quick, neat, and efficient as a judge trial, but, remember, our forefathers believed it is more important that we acquit a guilty person from time to time than convict an innocent person.

> Robert Vial, National President
> American Board of Trial Advocates
> Encino, California

Judges, by their very nature, are part of "the system" and (unlike jurors) are more likely to be swayed by the arguments of the state rather than those of some poor devil who is on trial because he was the first person the police tripped over when they went looking for someone to blame.

> David Hovgaard
> Castro Valley, California

It may also surprise many people to learn that early jurors in England were actual witnesses to the crime or at least had firsthand knowledge of it, such as doctors who treated the wounds of the accused or the victim. Over time, this evolved into the American system today, in which no juror knows anything whatsoever about the case.

Another mistaken notion is that juries are required to be of our "peers." (And we should be grateful this is not so; imagine who would be the peers of most defendants in the criminal courts.) Instead, juries must simply be representative of the community. (The phrase "by the lawful judgment of his peers or by the law of the land" appeared in the thirty-ninth article of the Magna Carta in the year 1215, but it doesn't appear in the United States Constitution. Instead, we are guaranteed "due process of law," including "trial by jury.")

In one survey of 7,000 jury trials, the judges disclosed the decisions they would have made if they had been jurors themselves, and it was discovered that they and the jury agreed in only 78 percent of all of the cases where a verdict was reached. (This includes both convictions and acquittals.) Of the remaining 22 percent, the judges would have convicted the defendants in nearly all of the cases (19 percent), but the jury had acquitted.

That remaining 22 percent (about 1,540 people) is the group that should concern us. In summary, out of those 7,000 jury trials, the judge would have freed 210 defendants whom the jury convicted. And the judge would have convicted 1,330 defendants that the jury freed. This is a serious discrepancy. Surely those 1,330 defendants were not set free because the jury viewed them as victims of government oppression or persecution.

I believe the O. J. Simpson trial—because of its extreme example and high visibility—has enlightened many of us about the weaknesses and flaws in our judicial system. Perhaps that raised consciousness will bring about needed change, whatever it may be—whether it's more juries that are not required to be unanimous to reach a verdict or panels of judges who can vote in accord with their consciences. Regardless, it seems clear that some change is due, and open discussion is the first step toward making that change become a reality.

Dear Marilyn:

Sometimes I think we're losing the fight against the decay in our society. I grew up in the 1970s, which seem very tame compared to the sexually permissive 1980s, and now in the 1990s, especially with the explosion of the drug problem, things look even worse. Does it seem very different to you, too?

Joanie Caldwall
Clearwater, Florida

Yes, it does, and the concerns of the past now seem very minor by comparison. In the 1970s, we watched the question, "It's midnight. Do you know where your children are?" flash on our television screens nightly. In the 1980s, it could have been "It's midnight. Do you know where your parents are?" But in the 1990s, it should be "It's midnight. Do you know where *you* are?"

Dear Marilyn:
    We have all witnessed the public campaign against smoking ciga-rettes. Why has there not been a similar campaign against drinking al-cohol? It would seem that many more deaths and health problems are related to alcohol than they are to tobacco. After all, we never hear that a smoking driver has run over a child.

Roy Anderson
Elmore, Alabama

There *has* been such a campaign, and it didn't work: Prohibition. But I do see your point—smoking seems to be a lesser social problem. However, this may explain why it's been easier to attack. Consider how difficult it would be to similarly tackle the real whoppers—like obesity. After all, what would we do? Outlaw the eating of junk food in pub-lic places? Insist that waiters refuse to sell desserts to people who are clearly obese? Why, the whole *country* would rebel!

Dear Marilyn:
    I have been adversely affected by certain land-use laws, but two dif-ferent legal firms have advised me that although my claims are certainly valid morally, they are legally void under existing state law. I'm not ask-ing you for a legal opinion in my own case, but am I being naive to ex-pect that laws should meet moral standards? Or can't we expect the law to be moral?

R. L. Wiggins
Portland, Oregon

Most laws in a democracy *do* meet moral standards—that's one of the main reasons those laws exist. Legislators merely reflect people's concerns when they do what they are elected to do—create laws. Of course, this country's major elections are usually close calls, so nearly half of the electorate disagrees with the philosophy of those elected, but it's not usually a night-and-day moral difference, anyway.

Dear Marilyn:

You once wrote that most laws in a democracy meet moral standards and that's one of the main reason they exist. However, it has become "politically incorrect" to oppose something on moral grounds. Gambling comes to mind. If there are no more moral standards, does this mean we have lost all the basis for our laws?

C.K.
New Orleans, Louisiana

Not at all, even though I think we'll see increasingly creative interpretations of those laws. Regardless, I've found a simple way out of this dilemma, and I've practiced it myself over the last decade. Just examine your moral convictions and find their philosophical basis, instead.

For example, I dislike institutionalized gambling, but for intellectual reasons, not moral ones. One reason is that when we *lose* money gambling, which is very likely, it was a poor way to spend it. (We can't eat or wear tote tickets.) Another reason is that when we *win* money gambling, which is very unlikely, it was a poor way to "earn" it. (We learn nothing to enable us to duplicate the result.)

A third reason is that gambling encourages empty risk-taking behavior; it has no redeeming social or personal value if the risk is unsuccessful. (If we open a business instead, that's productive risk-taking; we contribute to society and gain valuable personal experience even if the business fails. We'll also be much more likely to succeed the next time around.)

And a fourth reason is that gambling seldom has redeeming social or personal value even if the risk is successful; nearly all of the time, we're the only beneficiary, and even then, the dollar amount is insignificant in the long run. (If we win an Olympic medal instead, we seldom earn a lot of money, but our country is proud of us, and our self-esteem soars.)

In short, take a good look at the philosophical underpinnings of most moral convictions, and you'll find broad foundations of good, solid thinking there.

Dear Marilyn:

How can we teach respect for law when law is just a matter of opinion, sometimes only a 5–4 opinion, and an opinion of people appointed for political reasons?

Howard M. Sage
Portland, Oregon

You make a good point, but respect has more than one meaning. One is "to esteem" and the other is "to avoid violation of." There are plenty of laws I believe are unwise, but I obey them anyway, and that's the sort of respect we must teach—that a law-abiding society is better than an outlaw society.

Dear Marilyn:

Is it worth standing up for something that you strongly believe in, when the consequence for standing up may be greater than what you accomplish by doing so?

J.M.V.
San Diego, California

Maybe. But there are times when it's better to shut up than to stand up.

Five

On Government

"I can't think of any greater harm
to humanity than the kind that's done by
good people who embrace a bad cause."

Dear Marilyn:
  What is the greatest mistake ever made?

                              Kelly Wrede Nacosté
                              Portland, Oregon

I can't think of any greater harm to humanity than the kind that's done by good people who embrace a bad cause. So perhaps the greatest mistake ever made is to not fully understand what you believe in.

Dear Marilyn:
  Do you feel that our government is operating in the manner that the writers of the Constitution intended?

                              Hall Cook
                              Maryville, Tennessee

The Constitution, yes. The government, no. But that shouldn't bother us. The founders of our country were mere mortals, not gods, and it doesn't make good sense to extend their intentions into a future that they couldn't possibly have foreseen, including everything from the rise of women to the information explosion. (Imagine any of today's leaders deciding how the country should be run in the year 2200.)
  But the Constitution itself has proved to be an extraordinarily fine document, serving to foster an impressive freedom and stability along with an equally impressive prosperity over the last two centuries of change, and we can certainly be grateful to them for that. (And it occurs to me that we would be lucky if today's leaders would just be able to figure out how the country should be run *now*.)

Dear Marilyn:
  Should I trust the government? If so, to what degree?

                              M. Nex
                              Oakland, California

Can you trust your neighbor? That is, can you trust your neighbor to make decisions about your life that are better than the decisions you would make yourself? If so, you can rest easy; if not, take note. Government is changing as democracy runs its course. It's becoming increasingly composed of ordinary people (like your neighbor) instead of heroes—men and women of extraordinary judgment who can protect us from ourselves. Those ordinary people may be highly skilled, well educated, or just plain likeable, but they're not visionaries.

This may be due to an inherent weakness in the process: in order to get elected, politicians are turning more and more to buying votes (sometimes innocently, but often not) with promises and programs that can do more harm than good. So the wisest people, who, by definition, always lead others instead of following them (because they have a *greater* vision, not the most *common* one), are having increasing difficulty getting elected. In short, I think you can trust government (like your neighbor) to have good intentions, but to be fallible about social issues and unrealistic about economic matters.

Dear Marilyn:
   In political terms, what is the different between freedom and liberty?
                                          G. Sanchez
                                          Fort Wayne, Indiana

Freedom can be defined as having no restraint; liberty can be defined as having no undue restraint. In political terms, then, the loss of complete freedom is the price we civilized people pay for liberty defined by law, which is a much better deal all around, especially when we consider what some folks might take it upon themselves to feel free to do otherwise.

Dear Marilyn:
   Where does the right of free speech end?
                                          C. B. Park
                                          Lynn Haven, Florida

We usually think of free speech as the ability to express disagreement openly, and that principle seems sound as far as it goes. But perhaps the right of free speech should end where dishonesty begins. The only problem is that it so often takes a Solomon to tell the difference between the two.

Dear Marilyn:

Someone once asked whether you could find a single flaw with majority rule, and you answered, "Yes. The majority may be wrong." But by whose standards?

                                        Bruce Blinder
                                        St. Paul, Minnesota

By the standards of the small number of extraordinary people whose understanding of humanity transcends the waxing and waning of ideological fashion and whose ethics preclude them from serving their own personal interests at the expense of the citizenry. These are the people of great stature—the best of us—who should be our leaders. That is, our leaders must never be ordinary people, or we'll have to accept the consequences of choosing quantity over quality. (As a minor example, imagine the results of majority rule in the classroom—whatever is the most common answer is the "right" one?!)

Dear Marilyn:

Which is better for citizens—running the state themselves when they refuse to be concerned with or informed on issues broader than their own personal concerns, or letting the state be run by a benevolent dictator who makes all the decisions?

                                        Bill Newton
                                        Escondido, California

Running the state ourselves is bad enough, but any totalitarian state would be worse. There are no benevolent dictators. If they were, they wouldn't need to dictate.

Dear Marilyn:

What's one of the best ways to judge a leader?

                                        Dan Murphy
                                        Wheaton, Maryland

Look at his followers.

Dear Marilyn:

After filling out dozens of applications to colleges, I've discovered there's a great deal of emphasis on "leadership." But isn't being a follower as worthy an occupation as being a leader?

Carolyn Wei
Seattle, Washington

Sure it is. Being a leader doesn't mean a person is right, good, or anything else. It just means he can get people to follow him. And colleges dearly love to have alumni whose names are famous. Wouldn't it be nice if they emphasized "character" instead?

Dear Marilyn:

Should I vote for a dishonest man with whose principles I agree?

Daniel Baralt
Tustin, California

No. For one thing, you can never know the principles of a dishonest man. But more importantly, if your principles actually do agree with his, maybe the time has come for you to question your principles.

Dear Marilyn:

If one can recover his public image only by admitting his mistakes, and politicians seldom do, please explain why they are reelected time after time.

Joe Smith
West Palm Beach, Florida

Because voters have just as difficult a time admitting their *own* mistakes.

Dear Marilyn:

Do you find ignorance necessary in maintaining emotional stability?

J.S.
Davis, California

Only when I'm watching C-SPAN.

Six

On Economics

"Your earning power is far
greater than your saving power."

Dear Marilyn:

Is the form of democracy now practiced in the United States capable of solving our immense problems, specifically the inability to match revenue to the ever-increasing demands for expenditure? Whom do you blame for our current dilemma, and what would you do?

Marco M. Budny
Lexington, Kentucky

In a way, I blame all the politicians who've tempted the voters with promises of funds and favors in order to get elected, but in another way, I blame the voters themselves. After all, it was we who elected the people who spent us into this mess. Moreover, increased taxation (of anyone—wealthy, middle class, or poor) only makes the matter worse because reducing the current budget deficit isn't as important as reducing the size of the budget itself, which may ultimately bankrupt us. So here's a new idea: we've all heard about every kind of economic reform except this one—"voter reform." How about encouraging people to learn more about how our government works before they cast another ballot?

I'd focus on economic education as a civic obligation for all Americans who want to cast a responsible vote. As a people, we know very little about elementary economics, and that innocence is showing in the voting booth, which has great impact on both our public and personal financial stability and opportunity.

Nearly all of us could benefit from a better understanding of economics. In 1988, according to the *New York Times*, "More than half of all high school students in a national survey could not define basic economic terms like profit and inflation. . . . only 25 percent gave the correct definition for inflation, 34 percent knew that profits equal revenue minus costs, and 45 percent could identify the term 'government budget deficit.'" A press release from the Joint Council on Economic Education quoted Paul Volcker, former chairman of the board of the Federal Reserve System, as saying, "While *interest* in matters of economics runs high in American minds, their *understanding* of the subject lags far behind their counterparts in other industrialized countries."

This situation appeared unchanged four years later. In an overview of a national survey of American economic literacy conducted jointly in 1992 by the National Center for Research in Economic Education and the Gallup Organization, it was noted that "All survey respondents had strong opinions about economic issues despite the fact that they often had very limited economic knowledge about an economic issue."

The study assessed high school seniors, college seniors, and the general public, discovering that, for example, "the economic issue of greatest concern was unemployment. The respondents in all groups recommended a number of actions that should be taken by the federal government to reduce unemployment; yet, only about a fourth or less of each group knew the current national rate of unemployment." Also, "The general public suggested a number of actions to be taken by the federal government to reduce the federal deficit, but less than a quarter of each group knew the size of the deficit or could define a budget deficit." In addition, "Only a quarter of high school students, a third of the general public, and about half of college students knew that the Federal Reserve was responsible for monetary policy. Even fewer could recognize an example of monetary policy, but a large majority of each group thought some organization other than the Federal Reserve should be responsible for conducting monetary policy."

In that overview of the national survey of American economic literacy conducted jointly in 1992 by the National Center for Research in Economic Education and the Gallup Organization, it was also noted that "These results suggest that, for most people, the knowledge base for understanding or discussing most economic issues is inadequate. *This economic illiteracy has the potential to misshape public opinion on economic issues and lead to economic policies that have negative or perverse effects on the economy.*" The year 1992 was a major election year, and the campaigns focused on the economy.

The survey itself states that "The American public, high school seniors, and college seniors show widespread ignorance of basic economics that is necessary for understanding economic events and changes in the national economy. When asked questions about fundamental economics, only 35 percent of high school seniors, 39 percent of the general public, and 51 percent of college seniors gave correct answers." For example, "Only 22 percent knew the current national rate of employment; of those who gave a response, most thought the rate was much higher than it was." And, "Only 11 percent knew the current national rate of inflation."

And who knew what? Among the most interesting findings were the following:

"In general, males scored higher than did females within each of the groups surveyed. Receiving the highest average scores were male college seniors. High-school-senior females and general-public females received the lowest scores.

"Political conservatives received higher economic knowledge scores than did middle-of-the-road or liberal respondents. This was the case in each of the groups included in the survey.

"Economic knowledge was also found to be related to respondent's level of income. Wealthier respondents received higher average scores in terms of economic knowledge than did persons with lower incomes.

"The current projections call[ed] for a $400-billion deficit in the Federal budget for the 1992 fiscal year (October 1, 1991, to September 30, 1992). About two-thirds of the respondents in each group thought the deficit would be $700 billion or $1 trillion. In fact, 43 percent of the general public, 43 percent of the high school seniors, and 48 percent of college seniors thought the Federal deficit would be about $1 trillion.

"Profits as a percentage-rate return on investment have averaged about 13 percent for most major American corporations over the past decade. On the average, the general public thought that American corporations made approximately 32 percent profit as a return on investment."

We owe it to our country to educate ourselves before we vote. Casting a thoughtful vote is a duty for all citizens, and an uninformed vote is worse than no vote at all. Whether we're going to cast our vote or run for office ourselves, sound economic understanding is the heart of good government, and what this country needs, more than anything else, is better government. I think we should encourage people to vote on "the honor system." That is, if we know we can cast an informed vote, we should be sure to do so. But if we know we can't, we should consider staying away from the polls until we're ready for that very serious civic responsibility. Those who cast thoughtless votes contribute to the problem that this great country needs so much to cure.

Dear Marilyn:

I have a budget for my income and credit-card charges, etc., which means I am in debt. Can you relate my income and indebtedness compared to the national income and debt?

D. C. Adams
Fresno, California

Let's suppose you have an income of $125,760 that comes not from work, but instead from the contributions of all your friends and relatives who work. You're not satisfied with what $125,760 can buy this year, so you prepare yourself a budget of $146,060 and charge the $20,300 difference to your credit card, on which you're already carrying an unpaid balance of $452,248, boosting that to $472,548, on which you pay interest daily. Multiplied ten million times, that's what our government did in the fiscal year of 1994.

Dear Marilyn:

How do you feel about this reasoning? I read that most government agencies on a budget will go to great lengths to deplete that budget—our tax dollars—by the end of the year so that it will remain the same or be increased for the next year. I've even seen organizations *squander* money this way. Shouldn't they try to *save* taxpayer money instead of *spend* it?

Roger Simpson
Newport News, Virginia

I believe their reasoning is sound because saving taxpayer money is not one of the primary goals of a governmental agency. Even spending it *wisely* is not a primary goal (although it may be a secondary one). Instead, the intent is to spend tax dollars to accomplish a particular political goal, and if an agency hits that target, it fulfills its mission. This is where your point highlights the apparent paradox. Agencies that fulfill their missions are no longer needed, so in order to keep their jobs, these folks never seem to finish. This is why government programs, once launched, remain in the budget "forever," become institutionalized, and drive the need for an increasing amount of tax dollars. The phenomenon works fairly well in the beginning of a program, when much can be accomplished with comparatively little money, but in later years, the reverse slowly becomes the case: more and more is spent to accomplish less and less.

Dear Marilyn:

Why must everyone have a percentage increase in wages, etc., every year? Can it mathematically be proven that we cannot afford this national practice because the effects of compounding the percentages upward can only end in financial disaster?

Hugh Adams
Nicholasville, Kentucky

When we add increasing prices to this scenario, we have the classic description of the "inflationary spiral," which is serious enough. But the mathematical consequences also have been producing an increasing *income tax* burden of which few citizens are aware. That is, when we increase the tax rates of those making more than we do, we increase them for ourselves and our children. Call it "tax inflation." Because tax rates were raised on upper-income citizens in previous years, middle-income citizens are saddled with those rates now. (And the same for middle-income and lower-income folks.) Here's how the math works.

Say Tom earns $18,200 in taxable income and pays $3,565 in federal taxes. His effective tax rate is 20 percent ($3,565 ÷ $18,200 = 20 percent). In the next bracket, Dick earns $23,500 and pays $5,367 in federal taxes. His tax rate is 23 percent ($5,367 ÷ $23,500 = 23 percent). In the next bracket, Mary earns $28,800 and pays $7,434 in federal taxes. Her tax rate is 26 percent ($7,434 ÷ $28,800 = 26 percent).

An inflationary four years pass. Because of the typical wage increases, let's say that the taxpayers in the lower two brackets earn the following salaries: Tom (raised from $18,200) now earns $23,500, and Dick (raised from $23,500) now earns $28,800. (Mary and taxpayers in higher brackets move up in salary likewise.)

But inflation has eliminated any actual gain, and real purchasing power remains just about the way it was before the four years had passed. (In real life, purchasing power often *drops,* making the situation even worse.) Tom and Dick didn't have exactly the same percentage gains—that's normal—but they think they must be stable because their salaries increased at least in rough proportion to the inflation rate.

They're dead wrong. Tom and Dick (and Mary and others) have silently floated into higher tax brackets. Even though their purchasing power is the same, Tom no longer pays 20 percent of his income (that is, his purchasing power) in taxes; he now pays 23 percent. Dick no longer pays 23 percent of his income in taxes; he now pays 26 percent. (And so on with higher brackets). In short, taxes have gone *up.* (By the way, this is not a fictitious example intended only for purposes of illustration; the tax brackets of Tom, Dick, and Mary were the actual tax brackets in place for individual unmarried taxpayers in 1980.) This is not to say that wages should not have been increased—only that if all tax rates are not continually reduced, people become worse and worse off.

Combine this with tax increases and deficit spending, and the situation eventually becomes impossible. In 1914, when the income tax first began, less than half of 1 percent of the population was required to pay any income tax at all, and those people paid only a few percent at most. State and local income taxes, which are also bracketed, aggravate the problem.

Dear Marilyn:
I have often heard that a flat tax is the fairest system. Would a flat tax of 10 percent generate enough revenue to allow government to bankroll necessary programs?

Robert C. Nelson
Los Angeles, California

A flat tax eliminates the tax inflation that occurs when earnings (but not purchasing power) escalate numerically into higher brackets. It also appears fairer in other ways. But when speaking of a flat tax of 10 percent, for example, which would generate less revenue than we have now, the question that arises first in many minds is whether the government can run so economically. To answer that, we might consider the experience of Hong Kong. In 1995, 58 percent of its residents paid no income tax at all (the rest paid up to 15 percent) because of *surplus* funds in the treasury—which remained even after government spending on public housing, transportation, and aid to people in need. Also in 1995, Hong Kong's per capita income surpassed that of the United Kingdom. Business is actively encouraged, regulation is kept to a minimum, and unemployment is just over 3 percent.

Contrast this with the situation in Spain, where unemployment reached 23 percent in 1995, the highest in Europe. Only ten years before, the economy was booming and the new socialist Prime Minister undertook to provide free health care and deep subsidies for college education for all citizens, and even forced businesses to provide lifetime contracts for their employees. Tax rates began to climb and escalated every year over the next decade, far surpassing those in the United States. Government and organized labor became virtual partners, and spending on social goals doubled before it all began to collapse. Foreign investment plummeted, and big business fled. What the future holds is still uncertain.

Dear Marilyn:

What are your thoughts on a national sales tax to replace income tax entirely?

Art Heinrich
Gaylord, Minnesota

In my opinion, it's a worthwhile concept and should be studied, but the ramifications of a change of this magnitude are so powerful and are so inherently unknowable (not just unknown) that I personally would not support such a tax at this time.

A national "consumption tax" (as opposed to a national income tax) would appear on the surface to have many positive aspects. Everything relating to the income tax would disappear overnight. No more withholding tax; no more record-keeping. People could sell homes, stocks, and other assets with no capital-gains tax. Nor would there be any tax on interest or dividends. With inheritance income taxes gone, no one would have to sell their parents' belongings in order to pay the taxes.

There are also many negative aspects. Everything we purchase would have a stiff sales tax added. All the poor people who pay no income tax now would receive no financial benefit from elimination of the income tax, but they'd still be faced with higher bills on their purchases. And all the people with after-tax cash in their savings accounts would find they'd have to pay tax all over again when they go to spend any of it.

But the most important negative aspect of all may be inherently unknowable. That is, how might we react to a national sales tax of, say, 15 percent? Relatively modest changes in our incomes (either up or down) produce great behavioral changes, including changes in our spending patterns. With an entirely new tax system, it's very unlikely that we would go on living (and spending) as before. But what would happen? Would we begin to spend more? Or would we begin to save everything we could for a few years in order to be free of taxes, watching our bank accounts grow at an unprecedented rate (at least since the income tax was instituted shortly after the turn of the century)? If we suddenly stopped spending, businesses would go bankrupt, and unemployment would shoot up. In short, even small economic changes have great ripple effects; a switch to a national sales tax instead of a national income tax is so fundamental that the risk would be enormous. I, for one, would not take that risk.

Dear Marilyn:

When I asked my tax man about a flat-rate tax system, he said that we could not have a fair tax and a simple tax at the same time. What could be fairer than a tax where lower-, middle-, and upper-income citizens pay the same rate?

Everett Harvey
Martinsville, Indiana

With our current system, tax rates rise as income does. One person making only twice as much as another may pay four times as much in taxes. This is clearly unfair—we don't require some people to pay four times as much for a fast-food hamburger as other people do. But there's no reason to call even a flat tax rate "fair." One person making twice as much as another would still pay twice as much in taxes. In other words, if we don't think middle-income people should pay twice as much for the same hamburger as lower-income people, we shouldn't think it fair for them to pay twice as much for the same government services.

And of course we can have a fair tax and a simple tax at the same time. Isn't the cost of that hamburger both fair and simple? It's the same for everyone. Or would your tax man think that hamburgers should cost different amounts for different people, depending on their income? But just because some tax structures are unfair doesn't mean they're inherently wrong. Life is pretty darned unfair, too.

Furthermore, no responsible person would now advocate that we should change to a system whereby everyone pays the same dollar amount (not percentage) per person. Our government has grown so large (since the days when there was no income tax at all) that the average person couldn't afford to pay enough, and if the tax bill were set low enough for everyone, the government would go bankrupt, instead.

Dear Marilyn:

You once said, "Our government has grown so large (since the days when there was no income tax at all) that the average person couldn't afford to pay enough [if all taxpayers paid the same dollar amount, not percentage], and if the tax bill were set low enough for everyone, the government would go bankrupt, instead."

Many people believe that the government is already bankrupt, with a staggering debt of over $4 trillion that increases every year. Do you see any way, taxes or otherwise, that our government can ever get out of debt? Or do we just continue down this road to ruin and the eventual total collapse of our government and of life as we know it?

Howard Deevers
Monroeville, Pennsylvania

Given the political realities of the situation, I don't see a way out without broad-based changes in our way of social thinking. Higher taxes (including income taxes, sales taxes, and the like) treat the symptoms only temporarily, and they make the disease (of extravagant government spending) worse. I think the situation can be cured if we can get our money back into our own hands to spend wisely and stop allowing our politicians, both national and local, to buy votes with it; the problem is that those very votes are numerous enough to maintain the current situation while the rest of us stand helplessly by.

In addition to buying votes, what's wrong with government doing the spending instead of us doing the spending ourselves? In short, consider this. When you spend your own money on yourself (such as buying yourself a tie or a handbag), you do an excellent job of keeping the cost down and getting exactly what you want. But when you spend your own money on someone else (such as buying a gift tie and handbag for your parents), you still keep the cost down, but you don't get them what they'd choose themselves. (Think about all the gifts you've ever received; what percentage of them would you have chosen yourself?) Even worse, when you spend a third party's money on someone else, you not only don't get the recipient what he or she would choose, there's no pressure to keep the cost under control. (Imagine being allowed to charge that gift tie and handbag to "the taxpayers" instead of to your own account; would you worry about the cost?) This is what the government does, and in a massive way, every single day.

❌

Dear Marilyn:

In our society, there are lower-income people, middle-income people, rich people, millionaires, and even billionaires. How much money must a person have in order to be considered "rich"?

Martin Halpern
Boca Raton, Florida

It's no wonder there's such disagreement these days about who's rich and who's not. That's because the term "rich" is one of those words that often tell us much more about the *speaker* than about the person being described. In brief, it's a derogatory term for people who make more money than the speaker himself or herself wants them to make—for reasons that range from outright envy to simple innocence about what money can buy. If the reason is closer to envy, the speaker calls people "rich" when they surpass about $100,000 in yearly income; if the reason is closer to innocence, the speaker calls people "rich" when they approach $200,000 in yearly income. So I'd say the "rich" range begins somewhere between $100,000 and $200,000 in the eyes of the people who use the word.

But this range is objectively incorrect. We've used the terms "rich" and "millionaire" for so long that we've forgotten what inflation has done to the value of a dollar. Around the turn of the century, a millionaire was indeed wealthy relative to other Americans. This is no longer the case. Consider what has happened to *prices.* In 1900, you could buy a pair of men's work shoes for $1.25, a square yard of carpeting for 12¢, and a hundred pounds of salt for 20¢. According to my figures, it now takes at least $25 million to live the way $1 million used to provide. And if you include our current income tax rates, you'd need nearly $50 million to feel as wealthy in 1995 as a millionaire used to feel in 1900.

Dear Marilyn:

Do you think it's true that the wealthy have money because they don't spend it, and the poor do not have money because they *do* spend it? When people say this to me, I find it very irritating.

Linda Gittinger
Columbia, South Carolina

No, I don't think that's true at all, and this myth can cause great frustration in those who try to save as much as they can. While saving money is a basic component of a responsible lifestyle, no one becomes wealthy by saving; people become wealthy by *earning*. There's an upper limit to the number of dollars that we can save, no matter how much we try, and the closer we get to that limit, the harder it gets.

For example, look at your electric bill. Let's say you use energy freely, and your bill is $100 a month, which you believe is too high for you. So you take all the obvious steps to reduce that, such as changing the setting on your thermostat, and you manage to get your bill down to $70. Then you take the less-obvious steps, such as reducing the wattage of your light bulbs, and you get the bill down to $50. And then you take even-less-obvious steps, such as taking lukewarm baths instead of hot ones, and you get the bill to $40. But try as you might, that bill isn't going to budge much more unless you don't mind reading by candlelight. And even if you eliminate your electric bill entirely, you'll save only $100 a month. In short, your *earning power* is far greater than your *saving power.*

Dear Marilyn:

Because of my professional interests, I am destined to a life of poverty, but I wonder about the salaries commanded by athletes and show-business folks and big businessmen. How much money is really enough for one person or family?

Tim Whisenand
Tonopah, Nevada

It depends on our political climate. In a forcibly egalitarian society like the former Soviet Union, "enough" was reached when no one had any more than anyone else. One party official was denounced when he was caught with the spoils of corruption hidden in the trunk of his car—a crate of oranges and a ham. But here in this country, the sky's the limit. Or do you think we should outlaw lotteries that have a prize of more than, say, a million dollars?

Dear Marilyn:

Whenever I read about popular actors and how much money they make per film, I am outraged! I appreciate good entertainment and all the hard work that people like Madonna or Michael Jackson do, but don't you think it's a little crazy? I also see how many of them are very political. How come they don't give *their* money away to homeless people and the elderly?

Pam Wood
Indianapolis, Indiana

It looks hypocritical, doesn't it? But we must keep in mind that these people lose half their income to taxes (as do all other wealthy people), and so they're already giving more to the government than everyone else. That factor aside, I do know what you mean, but it's our own fault. We complain about the price of a fifteen-dollar vaccine against smallpox, surely one of the best buys in the history of the planet, but willingly pay fifteen dollars for a new compact disc. That is, our current culture finds it ethically acceptable to profit from such activities as singing and dancing, but morally distasteful to profit from developing products like new pharmaceuticals and medical diagnostic tools. Unless this attitude changes, empty entertainment may continue to assume an expanding role in an increasingly superficial society.

Dear Marilyn:

Which makes the most money—selling a product at a high price so that only a few people can afford it, or selling a product at a low price so that many people can afford it? I suppose the ratio of rich versus poor is a factor.

Gladyce Ankerson
Traverse City, Michigan

Your profit depends far less on the ratio of rich versus poor than it does on your competition. In a free market, the price of your product can be successfully set only as high as the quality (including desirability and need) will bear. If you set your price higher than that, the competition will put out a comparable product at a lower price. But should the competition put out that product at only a slightly lower price or a very much lower one? If their expenses are high, the price would need to remain relatively high, but if expenses are low and they keep the price relatively high, more competition will put out a comparable product at a lower price again. This process tends to continue until the price is as low as quality and expenses warrant. Costlier products will have to be better in quality in order to be successful. It all makes good sense, it makes good products, it makes money for employers and those they employ, and this is one of the places where our country's system of free-market capitalism gets such a fine reputation.

Dear Marilyn:

If you sat ten people down at a poker table with a stake of one hundred dollars each and told them to play nonstop, eventually one person would have one thousand dollars, and the other nine would be broke. It seems to me that that's the way our economic system works—the rich get richer.

My plan is to confiscate the wealth and assets of all corporations and individuals and redistribute it equally among all our citizens. Sort of like a giant monopoly game—we clear the decks every fifty years or so and start all over again. If we did that today, how much money would I end up with?

Charles Chandler
Whitesboro, Texas

I don't know, but it doesn't matter—your currency would be worthless because our entire economic system, based and built on capitalism, would be destroyed. Also, your plan has already been tried, and it was an unmitigated disaster. (You can ask Mikhail Gorbachev for the details.) Most importantly, though, given your implication that economic equality is a philosophical goal and not simply a spiteful or self-serving one, what is your moral justification for limiting the confiscation and redistribution to this country?

Dear Marilyn:

I have a "no annual fee" credit card, and I always pay the charges in full and on time, so there's no interest, either. I'm happy with the convenience, but I figure the credit-card companies aren't in business for my convenience; they're in business to make money. Are they making any money from me, and if so, how?

Gary Cummings
Bridgewater, New Jersey

The credit-card companies are selling this convenience to the merchants with whom you do business by charging them a percentage fee every time the credit card is used. Fees vary widely, but 3 percent is common. Some merchants love credit cards, but others detest them, depending on whether credit-card usage brings enough increased business or just added expense. Surely, it raises prices to some extent, but so do other conveniences like parking lots. Even air-conditioning raises prices. The credit-card companies take a lot of bashing, but I don't think they deserve it any more than, say, the people who install and maintain escalators and elevators. If they weren't providing a welcome service, their use wouldn't have soared over the last few decades the way it has.

Dear Marilyn:

I'm totally furious about the new gas tax. We already pay about $1.11 a gallon at the pump for self-serve regular unleaded in this country, more here in Connecticut. What do *you* think about all this?

Jeffrey Wheeler
Winchester, Connecticut

I don't like the gas tax any more than you do, but let's keep the price of gasoline in perspective. In this country, a gallon is equal to 3.785 liters. The last time I bought a liter of soda, I paid $1. This means that the price of soda, which nearly everyone drinks and nearly no one complains about, is around $3.79 a gallon. At $1.11 a gallon, the price of gas, which is clearly far more valuable than soda, is only a third of that. It's something to keep in mind.

Dear Marilyn:

Aren't the American people entitled to a universal health-care plan equal to what is provided to the U.S. Congress?

Thomas Sheehan
Boynton Beach, Florida

Not by the logic you cite. The rest of us aren't entitled to office space, administrative assistants, and salary. Why should we be entitled to the government employees' health-care plan?

Dear Marilyn:

The individual with the highest IQ should address these questions. Why isn't the medical world helping us prevent diseases that are clearly avoidable? Doctors certainly possess the intellect to advance an effective strategy to eliminate this unnecessary expense. Are they constrained from doing so by their dogma? And why has the debate over reform paid so little attention to the health-care industry's profiting at our expense?

> Warren Smith
> Monument, Colorado

How would *you* go about reforming health care?

> J.P.
> Akron, Ohio

Doctors have been nagging their patients to take better care of themselves for as long as their profession has existed. Short of our best friends and relatives, there is no one who tries harder to get us to stop smoking, reduce our drinking, lose weight, and exercise more. The medical community has even provided us with an array of vaccines, available either at no cost or for less than the price of a pair of tennis shoes. It's hard to imagine how we could expect our doctors to do more—they *already* sound like Mom and Dad when we visit. Even if the government took over and required health clubs to admit all Americans regardless of their ability to pay, would we exercise any more?

Here are three important problems with medical-care costs:

- First, there is no free market in health care as there is with other necessities such as food, clothing, and shelter. Most spending is done by insurance companies, including the federal government's immense Medicaid and Medicare programs. Because people can buy without restraint, spending explodes. Imagine being able to purchase food, clothing, and shelter this way.
- Second, the health-care market is more regulated than any other market. As quality has floated heavenward, so have prices, but unnecessarily so. With far-less-costly regulation, this country's food, clothing, and shelter are *also* without parallel.

- Third, the health-care market is the only one to be successfully captured by the political doctrine that maintains all people should be equal. Envision the expense of providing only the finest restaurants, fashions, and homes to every citizen in an effort to equalize food, clothing, and shelter.

If the federal government takes over medical care, here is how these problems will become much bigger:

- One, personal involvement—even of one's insurance carrier— would virtually cease to exist.
- Two, regulation would be nearly total.
- Three, equality would be legislatively enforceable.

Health-care spending now accounts for about one-seventh of our economy, and the demand for goods and services appears limitless. The ability of health-care professionals to provide increasingly successful vaccines, treatments, and cures also appears limitless. In fact, in a free market, there could be no better a scenario as this one. Businesses and economies *thrive* on increasing sales.

What went wrong with health care? With too much government involvement and too little consumer education, we've disconnected this vibrant industry from the free market. If this is the case, there is a relatively simple solution that not only would achieve much of the political goal; it would even help health care blossom. In no other industry would we complain about virtually unlimited sales expansion combined with equally unlimited product-improvement potential. This is a *boom* scenario.

The skyrocketing of health-care costs is partly an illusion; actually, we've witnessed a skyrocketing of *desires* caused—understandably—by the awesome variety of goods and services that have arrived on the market over the last half of this century. If the only health care available now were the same as the health care available in the 1950s, we'd be far less interested. In this context, saying that the cost of health care has soared is like saying that the cost of dining out has soared because so many better (and more expensive) restaurants have opened in town.

Health-care professionals have brought us wonders, and we're buying them at a more rapid pace than any other time in history. But instead of being pleased that these wonders are available, we've become displeased at the thought of not being able to afford them all. This is understandable. Fine health care is more important than fine food. But that's what makes it so illogical when we criticize the cost. Some of the same people who will pay $15 for dinner will also complain bitterly about the price of vaccine. Consider buying a lifetime's protection against polio for only $15. That's also the price of a new compact disc. Which is the better buy? (But which gets the criticism?) Or consider the surgery that saves our life for $15,000. That's the price of a new automobile. Which is the better buy? (But which gets the criticism?)

We've all heard critics arouse us with complaints about medication that sells for a dollar but costs only pennies to manufacture. Let's apply that logic elsewhere. For example, what about that $10 fast-food dinner we had last night? How much does a chicken cost? And this doesn't take into account the fact that the average new drug costs $400 *million* to develop before it gets to the marketplace. It doesn't cost *anything* to develop a chicken! (Also, it takes about twelve years to bring a new drug to market, but because patient coverage ends in seventeen years, pharmaceutical companies have only five years to recoup their investment.)

Does the health-care industry profit at our expense? Yes. And so does just about every other industry, including farming (food), garment manufacturing (clothing), and building (shelter). As we earn money and then spend it, everyone profits at the expense of everyone else. That's what capitalism is all about.

Following is a ten-point outline for health-care reform:

- Deregulate insurance companies so they can sell policies with much higher deductibles, and educate consumers to understand why low-deductible policies are actually budget plans instead of the simple safeguards against unforeseen catastrophe that all policies once were. Paperwork, administrative costs, and profits for insurance companies may constitute 25 percent of health-care costs overall.
- Deregulate health-care forces that are competitive. For example, Certificate-of-Need regulations require that no more goods or services be provided in an area unless proved to be absolutely necessary. (So physicians can't perform, say, too many expensive CAT scans when machine time is strictly limited.) But this contradicts all free-market experience. Scarcity creates high prices

that will even *increase* according to demand. It is *abundance* that lowers prices. Radios, videocassette recorders, and computers all plummeted in price—*and* became increasingly sophisticated—as they became plentiful and manufacturers competed with each other. (So when CAT scanners become as plentiful, everyone will be able to afford CAT scans whether they need them or not.) That is, competition drives quality up and prices down.

- Deregulate insurance companies so they can sell a variety of customized policies ranging from no-frills coverage to luxury coverage, all tailored to individual and family desires, much in the same way that food, clothing, and shelter are on the market. People who don't want coverage for acupuncture, herbal medicine, hairpieces, drug abuse, and marriage counseling wouldn't have to pay for it the way many do now. Even important categories such as childbirth coverage and AIDS coverage could become optional.

- Provide incentives for health-care professionals (such as hospitals) to advertise so they can market plain-to-fancy goods and services both to insurance companies and directly to the consumer who has no insurance. We can have both perfectly acceptable (and lower-cost) medicine *and* highly sophisticated medicine, the way we have both fast food and fine food. In other words, highly sophisticated medicine costs far more for little additional value and people would be free to choose it if that's the way they want to spend their money (via expensive insurance or their own wallets), but it would be wasteful to provide it as a matter of course.

- Reform Medicaid and Medicare so that the government must reimburse individuals for expenses directly and may not conduct behind-the-scenes negotiations with health-care providers that give government a whopping discount and inflate the bills for the rest of us.

- Deregulate insurance companies and change the tax laws so companies can once again sell policies that are guaranteed to be renewable, regardless of health or employer, like health-insurance policies in the 1950s.

- Deregulate insurance companies and change the tax laws so companies can offer "coverage from conception" or "coverage from birth" as options—which would effectively cover every individual with all conditions if the mother chose it—and begin a campaign to educate future parents about why this expense should come before any other expense that is not a necessity for life. The great majority of children would likely be covered (as they are now). Of the minority that were not, nearly all would be healthy enough to be insurable at a later date. The remaining few who are uninsured and uninsurable could be covered by subsidized high-risk pools; twenty-eight states currently have them.

- Deregulate insurance companies so they can reject a new applicant for health-related reasons, freeing the companies for cost competition. According to the U.S. Department of Health and Human Services, these people (who have been rejected for insurance for medical reasons) currently total only 900,000—fewer than one-half of 1 percent of the population. These individuals would also be covered by subsidized high-risk pools.

    In the future, elective unborn- and newborn-coverage combined with guaranteed-renewable coverage has the potential to eliminate individuals who are otherwise uninsurable. But before that, if health care is allowed to become a free market, the price of goods and services may fall like the prices of cameras and televisions, putting ample care within reach of nearly everyone. In the meantime, however, a special government program for this particular living group could be piggybacked onto Medicaid for the rest of their lives only (no new individuals would be added after enactment of the law), serving as a temporary bridge to the new system.

- Educate consumers about why the purchase and maintenance of medical insurance should come before every nonessential purchase. (Nearly 40 percent of the uninsured have incomes over $30,000.) Social disapproval could be directed toward those who buy goods and services like cable television, restaurant meals, and vacations, but fail to purchase and maintain health-care insurance for themselves and their dependents.

- Allow Americans citizens to choose to be uninsured and spend their money on other things, if they wish. (There is a large young-and-healthy group already doing just that—nearly 60 percent of the uninsured are below the age of thirty.) For the vast majority of people, this will be perfectly acceptable. (About half of all health-care spending is on medical bills of $5,000 or less.) Also, hospitals are already required by law to treat emergencies regardless of ability to pay.

- And finally, numerous studies have shown that although people consume about 50 percent more medical care when it is totally free, as opposed to people who have a deductible of $2,000, this additional spending has no noticeable effect on health. Apparently, much of our health-care spending is a complete waste of time and money. This suggests that if the federal government expands "free" care, we will have even more waste than we do now and with no improvement in health. After all, we must remember that there is a distinct limit to how much we can improve our health with current technology, no matter how much money we spend on ourselves. If we have a head cold, spending a million dollars won't help us get better any faster, and if we have a terminal cancer, neither will a million dollars prevent us from dying.

My own health-insurance policy is guaranteed to be renewable for life, has no upper dollar limit to benefits, and has a $10,000 deductible. But I didn't choose this policy because I can afford to lose $10,000; I chose it because I wanted a change. I wanted protection only from real financial disaster; $10,000—which would barely buy an inexpensive automobile—doesn't qualify as a catastrophe. We don't feel that every new car sold in this country represents a financial disaster for someone.

Most folks to whom I've spoken about this policy (written by a major insurance company) think that because the guaranteed-renewable and no-maximum-benefit features are so desirable, it must be tremendously expensive. But that mistaken notion is the crux of the mathematical point of this column. The policy is *inexpensive*. It costs only *one-fifth* as much as my previous policy because it insures only the "high end" of expense (over $10,000) and doesn't cover the "low end" (under $10,000) like the previous one did.

Dear Marilyn:
My husband and I agree that it would take a genius to figure out which long-distance telephone company offers the most savings. Can you help us out?

Mollie L.
Vero Beach, Florida

I'm sorry to disappoint you, Mollie, but there are some questions that are just too darned tough!

Seven

On Political Correctness

"You can't even call someone 'spineless' anymore; you have to call him 'an invertebrate.'"

Dear Marilyn:
  Please explain just what it means to be "politically correct."

                                       Marilyn Waters
                                       Jackson, Michigan

Politically *polite* people take great care to voice only the opinions that are the least offensive to the most sensitive of the members of any identifiable group of people—especially in public—even when those opinions don't appear to have a sound basis in reality. Politically *correct* people actually *believe* all that nonsense. In other words, a politically polite person makes no comment when he meets a member of another ethnic group with a bizarre haircut; a politically correct person *compliments* him on it.

Dear Marilyn:
  Please distinguish the essential difference between a reasonable prejudice in human relations and an unreasonable one.

                                         Harry Greenwood
                                       Kapaa, Hawaii

Prejudice in human relations is now defined as inherently irrational, so these days there's no such thing as a reasonable prejudice. But if it weren't defined that way, I'd say that a "reasonable" preconceived notion is one that is based on common sense, broad experience, and an honorable nature.

Dear Marilyn:
  I would say that I have fairly liberal and feminist views. I was recently talking to two friends (of both sexes) who were against women and gays being in the military. My views are completely different, and although I know their opinion, it's very hard for me to respect it. How do you respect someone's opinion when it is based more on prejudice than on fact?

                                         Lauren Weldon
                                       Mechanicsburg, Pennsylvania

Speaking for myself, I don't try to respect all opinions—which are unsupported conclusions, after all—but for people who do (such as you) and who sometimes find it difficult, I'll offer this advice. Keep in mind that those people with whom you disagree may very well believe that *you* are the one with the unfounded judgment and that they are exercising tolerance when they put up with you. (For example, if a bartender refuses to pour a drink for a pregnant woman, is he guilty of prejudice?) Forget about the issue of the military for the moment. A firm conviction that only *you* know the facts shuts down the search for the truth about what makes sense, and that's what prejudice is all about.

Dear Marilyn:

I hope you can help me with something that has been bothering me for ages. Children are taught that the color black represents evil and white represents good. It's even in the movies—the bad guy wears black, and the good guys wear white. But if black is "bad," why do priests wear black?

LaTresa Jenkins
Fort Worth, Texas

I disagree with your premise. No one is taught that the color black represents evil. If you believe that, you're a prisoner of selective logic. Your own example of the priesthood illustrates the point. (Who represents saintliness more than members of the clergy? You may as well say that because priests wear black, children are taught that *black* represents good.) In other words, you can't generalize effectively from so minor a factor as old cowboy movies and the like, which often put light clothes on the lead character in order to make him stand out visually in the days of black-and-white film. Look at the broader context. What do people wear on the most serious occasions? Black. What do people wear to the most elegant social gatherings? Black. And what do people wear when they want to look the most important? Black. In short, Darth Vader wears black because it makes him look more powerful. Wimpy enemies aren't nearly so exciting to vanquish.

Dear Marilyn:

When you were asked about how children are taught that the color black represents evil and white represents good, you replied that you disagreed with the reader's premise and cited the fact that people wear black when they want to look their most elegant, important, or powerful. You even mentioned that priests, who surely represent goodness, wear black. But this symbolism is deeply rooted. Don't forget the "black plague" and how white symbolizes the purity of the bride, etc. I believe that the reader deserved a better-balanced answer.

Nell Ahl

Laurel, Maryland

Then let's not forget white elephants (items of dubious value), white-washing (hiding a misdeed), white-livered (being a coward), showing the white feather (behaving like a coward), waving the white flag (surrendering), and—from your own example—the "white plague" (tuberculosis).

And as far as the wedding party is concerned, why not note that the groom wears black? (Then again, if the bride wears white to symbolize her purity, maybe the groom wearing black makes good sense!)

Dear Marilyn:

As examples of racial stereotypes, how about the fear of darkness, which is "black," as opposed to the comfort of daylight, which is "white"? For example, I remember how my mother would begin to worry when it got dark.

Thelma

Jekyll Island, Georgia

Goodness. I should invent a word to describe our thinking these days. We're not just P.C.—politically correct; we're P.G.—politically *gullible*. It's time to develop a little backbone, Thelma! (Or you wouldn't even be able to call someone "spineless" anymore; you'd have to call him "an invertebrate.")

Dear Marilyn:

How "traditional" are the roles of breadwinner and homemaker? Didn't these roles originate only a century ago?

Carol Young
Worthington, Kentucky

For many centuries, men went *out* to work and women stayed *in* to work. That is, the family functioned as an independent unit. Women made raw food fit to eat, they fabricated clothing, and they taught children. The Industrial Revolution swept all that away. Factories processed food, textile mills made cloth, and public schools educated children. This opened the role of "housewife," in which middle-class women had more leisure than at any other time in history. (Upper-class women always had it; lower-class women never got it.) Despite the fact that housewives were busy with worthwhile endeavors, they clearly worked less hard than their earlier counterparts. Society considered this a privileged status and generally felt sorry for women who "had" to work. In sharp contrast, women today believe that equal status in the workplace is what they richly deserve, instead. So although the roles of breadwinner and homemaker go back to the beginning of civilization, the role of "housewife" may turn out to have existed only during that transition period between the time when men ruled the world without question and the time when men ruled the world *with* question!

Dear Marilyn:

I've read that Catherine Green invented the cotton gin, but because women were not allowed to apply for patents at that time, Eli Whitney took over the invention. If this is true, are there any records of other women inventors who received no credit or money for their inventions?

Deva Shama
Laguna Beach, California

I doubt very much that it's true. People have always fought over credit for inventions; for every one that is successful, there are dozens of people who claim it belongs to them instead. But don't blame the patent office for women's comparative absence there. Going all the way back to 1790, when Thomas Jefferson started it all, there has never been a restriction for sex, race, or anything else, for that matter.

Dear Marilyn:

Why did previous cultures give equal value to a queen and king but so little value to other women compared to men?

Dean Norman
Spartanburg, South Carolina

I don't quite agree with your premise. While queens wielded equal power, previous cultures insisted on fewer of them. As we know, it was usually the eldest son, not the eldest child, who inherited the throne. The eldest daughter was more of a compromise or caretaker, a person to whom the throne passed only by default when there were no "real" monarchs to inherit it. Even the relative value of their titles evidences this lower stature. Note that in England, for example, a reigning king's wife is usually given the title of "queen," but a reigning queen's husband is never given the title of "king," as with Queen Elizabeth and Prince Philip. That is, a queen consort (who is merely a spouse) has the same title as a queen regnant (who is actually a ruler). The title of "king" is held in much higher esteem and is reserved only for a reigning male—a "real" monarch.

Dear Marilyn:

The media are filled with articles about sexual harassment. I have also had discussions with male relatives regarding the confusion in men's minds as to what constitutes sexual harassment. What do *you* think about it?

Darlene Richman
Tooele, Utah

I've never been sexually harassed, but it's not because I haven't had experience with the behavior now called by that name legally. Over the course of my life, I've been hugged and kissed, heard cautious innuendo and bold propositions, and seen everything from amorous notes to bouquets of flowers delivered to my office. But it didn't bother me and still doesn't; sometimes I was indifferent, other times I was amused, but because most men are sincere, I usually enjoy their attention.

This is not to say that there aren't some real clods in the world, but criminalizing their behavior may cost us women more than we gain. When we say that we need the help of government to protect us from offense, we say that we're unable to handle the situation ourselves. And if we can't handle such ordinary matters as garden-variety office oafs, how can we maintain that we can handle academic, business, and governmental duties that routinely involve complex or brilliant or even dangerous men on the opposite side of the bargaining table?

Dear Marilyn:

I agree completely with your response to the question about sexual harassment. After becoming an employer myself, my conclusion is that there are a good number of women who have personalities inadequate to handle these things. I consider any woman who has the combined (typically female) traits of being submissive, tender-minded, and security-motivated, as inadequate for a job in business. Top it off with naiveté, and you have an individual who is easily manipulated, takes everything personally, and refuses to accept responsibility, even for herself! This is the perfect setup for sexual harassment to occur.

Barbara DeBaere Poppy
Madison, Wisconsin

Bravo! I'm confident that many people are as disgusted as I am with the women who want equality and yet demonstrate that they are not able to cope with the most common stresses of life.

Howard Hayes
Johnson City, Tennessee

I want to tell you that your comments about sexual harassment are the most sensible statement on the subject I have ever read. I can't believe this isn't stated more often.

Anna Robinson
Berkeley, California

Your article about sexual harassment is the greatest I have read from anyone at any time.

Tommy Smith
Dallas, Texas

At last! A sensible response to the question about sexual harassment. I wish your reply could be blown up to a full page and appear in every newspaper in the country.

Marie Williams
Sun City West, Arizona

I was disappointed in your response. Sexual harassment can be a frightening, possibly devastating experience. Please reconsider your position.

Nancy B. Weiler
Cheshire, Oregon

I am distressed about your reply. I respect you. How can you give such an answer? I suffered from trashy treatment, and today, two years later, I cannot trust any man. I have so much anger and rage inside me because of what happened.

Anonymous
Baton Rouge, Louisiana

I know of a woman who went to work when her husband died and needed to work with people she could trust. Instead, she encountered fear. She had always been treated with respect and could not handle her fear. She finally went to pieces emotionally and had to leave her job. It wasn't the crude, obnoxious clod that she couldn't handle. It was the fear. Please print this viewpoint in defense of all the women who have been sexually harassed and have lived with this fear.

Frances Lenz
St. Simon's Island, Georgia

Yes, women are unable to always handle such situations, and therefore society must protect them. I was harassed thirty years ago, and had I not run away from the situation, who knows what would have happened?

Joan Robbins
Oakland, California

Some women benefit from sexual-harassment legislation. However, this help comes at significant cost to the majority of women. Remember, we're not talking about rape. Instead, we're talking about social relationships, power games, and male dominance in the workplace. My point is that if a woman is frightened (and perhaps even devastated) by men who are inappropriately aggressive in as minor a matter as sex and in as safe a place as an office, how can she possibly hold a position of responsibility (such as the presidency) and handle a male aggressor with far more serious matters on his mind and nuclear weapons at his disposal? Such a woman can't. Sexual-harassment legislation reinforces the notion that most women are similarly weak. It recalls the time when women were provided cots in the workplace because they were thought prone to faint more.

Suppose a woman is in the armed forces, wants to be considered equal to the men there, and supports sexual-harassment legislation, both for herself and for others like her. How are we expected to believe that she can handle an enemy soldier when she herself feels that she can't even handle the guys who are on *her* side? So while we consider the benefits, we must also consider the costs. In short, we can't have it both ways.

Dear Marilyn:

A men's-rights group is going to use *Roe versus Wade* to sue for reproductive choice for men—the legal right to opt out of fatherhood. The group states that because the government cannot force women to be mothers, forcing men to be fathers should be declared unconstitutional. What do you think? Do the men have a point? If a woman has the legal right to opt out of motherhood, why can't a man have the legal right to opt out of fatherhood?

Debra Focht
Allentown, Pennsylvania

I sympathize with the many men who are trapped, but I think this point is weak. These men would not be opting out of fatherhood (by terminating a pregnancy); instead, they would be opting out of financial responsibility for the result of a pregnancy carried to term. Although women currently *do* have the right to opt out of motherhood (by terminating a pregnancy), they don't have the right to opt out of financial responsibility for a child who is born. So the comparison doesn't seem valid. (And a woman can't give up for adoption a baby that the designated father wants to keep; if he does, *she'll* have to pay child support. If no father was designated, no man was financially liable anyway.)

But these men have a stronger point they could use. Because nature didn't make men and women alike, it's impossible for the government to treat them that way. In other words, even if women have the right to end a pregnancy, men surely *never* will have the right to end one. The resultant "rights" inequity can be ended if men aren't involuntarily included by the government in the first place. That is, it would be fair to make fatherhood (with financial responsibility) a role to opt *into*, like women do, not a role to opt *out of.* This is a point that could be argued effectively.

Not that I'm arguing it myself, mind you. Once a pregnancy has begun, it's getting late in the game for concern over government-conferred rights. These days especially, unwanted pregnancies are so easily preventable that it's a shame we have so many to think about.

Dear Marilyn:

I just can't stand the custom of handing out pink announcements for newborn girls and blue ones for boys. (I mean things like those silly cigars with little colored bands.) In these modern times, why don't we treat both sexes alike right from the beginning?

                                        Marsha Rich
                                        Washington, D.C.

Because no new father wants the doctor to slap him on the back and say, "Congratulations! It's a baby!"

Eight

On Getting Ahead

"Being beaten is often a temporary
condition; giving up is what
makes it permanent."

Dear Marilyn:

Why is it so hard for people to get ahead in this world?

Oshelle Alexis Bobb
Brooklyn, New York

Because you can't "get ahead" without passing people—which means we can never all get ahead. And making matters even more difficult is the fact that we're all trying.

Dear Marilyn:

I understand that Abraham Lincoln suffered a nervous collapse before his presidency. Yet he went on to accomplish great things. Do you believe that many people who have a modest degree of mental illness can overcome their problems and achieve great things as well?

Anonymous
San Diego, California

Yes, I do, but I believe it's becoming increasingly difficult in modern times because we're labeling more and more personality factors as dysfunctional, disordered, and disabled. All the time we spend on our weak points is precious time lost in expanding our strong points. Unless we're really having trouble coping with everyday life, I suggest that for many of us, exploring our potential will enable us to achieve more great things than exploring our problems.

Dear Marilyn:

In a competitive world, whether it be among individuals, corporations, or nations, is it possible to have winners without also having losers? What should be the fate of the losers? What is our responsibility to them?

Joe Randles
Clearwater, Florida

In a way, it's not possible to have winners without also having losers, but we need not bemoan their fate, and one of our responsibilities may be to not feel sorry for them. Those who choose to compete, whether they win or lose, have improved themselves in the process. When we study to get into the school of our dreams, try to build an even faster computer, or launch telescopes into space, we're better off, not worse, and so is the world. So in a more important way, the "losers" are really winners, too.

Dear Marilyn:

I would like to know whether, in your opinion, it is more productive to "never give up" or to "know when you are beaten."

Jennifer Boulette
Sugarland, Texas

It has been my observation that being beaten is often a temporary condition; giving up is what makes it permanent.

Dear Marilyn:

If the maximum working hours were reduced from eight to seven, unemployment would drop to almost zero. Mathematically, would it work? I discussed this idea with an economics professor, and he agreed with me. So why do big industries fire good workers instead of reducing their working hours?

Sam Cater
Austin, Texas

I don't agree with you and the professor. Businesses couldn't slash unemployment by reducing working hours unless the current employees took a proportionate slash in their pay. Otherwise, where would the employers get the money to hire the new people?

Also, you're assuming that the unemployed are all willing and able workers, and that the capable ones should be able to find an appropriate job without delay, but that's not realistic. Even with the most benevolent of employers, people will still quit jobs for bad reasons, and others will get fired for good reasons. That is, there will always be movement in and out of the workplace in a free society. There's no reason to believe that the available job openings at any given time will happen to match the particular skills of the currently unemployed. An employer can't hire a carpenter to replace an electrician.

Dear Marilyn:

I'm unemployed at present, but it's embarrassing to admit it when people ask where I work. I know I'm a worthwhile person and that plenty of people don't always have jobs. You seem to know how to use logic to get the truth across. Do you have any suggestions about how I can tell the truth and yet not look bad?

Ed Mintz
Santee, California

Yes—in addition to looking for a job, do some volunteer work one day a week at a local nursing home or orphanage, help out at a halfway house or homeless shelter on a second day, and attend an adult-education course on a third day. Then you can face anyone and not only have plenty of fascinating things to talk about—you can first answer the question, "Where do you work?" with a big smile and say, "I'm gain-fully unemployed."

Dear Marilyn:

What's the best advice you can give to an eighteen-year-old, less-than-ambitious, jobless, lazy, high school graduate of a son?

Charles Ballard (the son)
Oakland, California

Go right back to school and study hard to get rid of those lazy habits and then run for political office, young man. A less-than-ambitious fel-low with your kind of honesty is just the sort of politician we need!

Dear Marilyn:

In your opinion, is it harmful to teach reading, math, and other skills to children before school age? That is, does being smarter or at least having more knowledge than other children cause a child to be an out-cast among his peers?

Lani Roberts
Las Vegas, Nevada

Based on my own observations, I'd say that if a child is brighter *and* has a likeable personality, he will be significantly more popular than average. However, if that child is unlikeable instead, he will be significantly *less* popular. The smarter the youngster, the more his personality affects his popularity, both positively and negatively.

Dear Marilyn:

An "F" is usually a grade below 60 percent or 70 percent. But why should we fail a student who has correctly answered *over half* the questions?

Carol Tiffin James
Rockvale, Tennessee

It appears that you're making the philosophical statement that if you're right more often than you're not, you shouldn't be considered a failure. That is, scores above 50 percent should be graded as successful (albeit to varying degrees) and scores below that should be graded as unsuccessful (again, to varying degrees). But this yes/no dividing line fails to distinguish the person who has successfully become *educated* from the person who has not. To illustrate the point, say you take a true/false test of one hundred questions in a subject about which you know nothing whatsoever. The test could even be in a language foreign to you. Just flipping a coin will get you a score of around 50 percent!

Let's take this to the extreme and say that a multiple-choice test has four answers per question. If you think that students should be passed who know the answer to over half the questions (50 percent), you'd have to add the 12.5 percent (one-fourth of the remaining 50 percent) that they'd get marked correct simply by guessing (with no knowledge at all). And even that low a standard still adds up to a pass/fail borderline of 62.5 percent for students to top.

Dear Marilyn:

Do you think grades would be increased among high school students if they were able to chose more of their classes—say, by their sophomore year—instead of being forced to take a certain number of classes that do not pertain to their interests or goals? (I never plan to trace another nerve from a frog's foot to his brain, although I was able to do it.)

Patrick Moseley
Frederick, Maryland

I do think grades would be higher, but that's not the point of education. Learning how to make your mind operate in a wide variety of disciplines actually enables it to operate better in just one area of specialty later on, even many of those that seem remote. For example, learning the rigorous logic of mathematics makes a far superior physician; learning the uncertainties of biological systems makes a far superior physicist; and learning the limits of physical science makes a far superior poet.

Dear Marilyn:

I hope you can resolve a long-standing battle with most everyone I know. Between watching television and reading, which do you believe is the more passive activity, and why? Most everyone firmly believes that reading is just as passive as watching television. I disagree. Regardless of the subject, if the material were to be read, wouldn't that be more stimulating and therefore less passive than to simply sit and watch it?

Shannan Catalano
Lake Havasu City, Arizona

For the most part, reading is far more active than watching television, even with the finest material. Envision yourself miserably ill some evening with a cold and headache. Which sounds less taxing? Reading Leo Tolstoy's *War and Peace* for four hours? Or watching Audrey Hepburn in the film version? When you read, your mind runs at full speed, deciphering the code we call written language and supplying imagery, passion, and pain. But when you watch television, it's all been done for you. The difference is like walking a few miles versus driving a car.

After all, activity and passivity aren't determined by the number of calories expended. You can take an active part in making a decision while sitting quietly at your desk, or you can passively accept a decision, outwardly behaving just about the same way.

Dear Marilyn:

I'm a college student working toward a second degree, and I spend most of my time attending classes, studying, and doing homework. Whenever I have free time, I'm always hesitant to read anything that's not specifically related to my fields of study. Somehow I feel that by reading something else, I might be subconsciously detracting from the material I'm trying to learn for my classes. I know that the human brain is capable of much more than we demand of it, so I'm wondering if this is a valid concern. If you think it isn't, should we try to absorb as much information as we can, or should we take in information naturally through reading, experience, and just being alive?

                                        Matthew Killinger
                                        Corvallis, Oregon

You sound like every instructor's dream student, as conscientious as you are bright. This may surprise you, but I think you're right to concentrate almost exclusively on your studies. Not only will it make them easier, you'll never have a better opportunity to learn about these subjects than you do now. But after leaving school for good, I'd relax and enjoy following my interests, if I were you, which would include my work, but not necessarily be dominated by it. (And if more students had your attitude, this country's future would brighten considerably.)

Dear Marilyn:

Can you give me any solid reason to try so hard to "be all you can be" the way we're always hearing?

                                        Jill Mackie
                                        Rosedale, New York

Yes—it's so you don't wake up one day to find yourself over the hill before you even got to the *top* of the hill.

Nine

On Nature

"Even a wise old owl doesn't have the foggiest notion that mating may produce little owlets, and he doesn't give a hoot, either."

Dear Marilyn:

In the ongoing discussion about the theory of evolution, two questions about science remain: (1) Does science seek the truth, even if the truth includes the existence of God? (2) Or does science only seek answers that first exclude any possibility that God is a part of the truth? A theory of our origins that eliminates the input of God is worthless if, in fact, God created everything.

Robert Forman
Lakewood, Colorado

I agree—such a theory would be worthless. And no scientist wants to spend his or her precious time on Earth formulating worthless theories. That's why I believe they would never exclude any possibility, especially the existence of a God. After all, they know that the first scientist who proves that God exists would be revered all over the planet.

Dear Marilyn:

I would like to know if it is illogical for a person to make the statement, "I am an atheist." How could anyone say they *know* there is no God?

Sandra Yerna
Port St. Lucie, Florida

The same way they say they "know" anything else—they judge the substance of what they see and hear, then draw a conclusion. If we had to know everything from firsthand experience, we'd "know" very little indeed. For example, we all know that the giant panda is endangered, but we base that conclusion entirely on outside sources of information. This is not to say that information cannot be erroneous or that we can't draw an incorrect conclusion. We can, we do, and we always will.

Dear Marilyn:

Paleontologists tell us that humans appeared on Earth millions of years after the dinosaurs had become extinct. If the theory of evolution is correct—and these two life forms did not overlap—how do you account for the Norse mythology of dragons that snort fire out of their nostrils, and heroes slaying them to save beautiful maidens?

Richard Rhodes II
St. Petersburg, Florida

Let's look at the dragons of Teutonic mythology in context. The main sources for our knowledge come from oral poems that were later written into two works called the *Eddas*. In them, the creation of life was described, beginning with a young giant named Ymir who arose from a great emptiness (Ginnungagap) between the land of fire (Muspellsheim) and the land of ice (Niflheim). A giant tree (Yggdrasil) supported all subsequent creation, and a giant serpent (Nidoggr) lived near its root. Note the fondness for giants, common to many other mythologies, and especially note the giant serpent. Enlarge most any common lizard found in Europe, and you'll get a creature that looks very much like a dragon or dinosaur.

Dear Marilyn:
Are there mistakes in Nature?

M. T. Horn
St. Louis, Missouri

Yes, they're common, and they're called "mutations," which are actually sudden, seemingly random, inheritable changes in the DNA sequences (which carry the genetic information). (For our purposes, let's label non-inheritable changes as "accidents" instead of "mistakes.") The result is an altered organism, and the alteration is seldom a positive one in complicated creatures such as human beings and other animals.

Dear Marilyn:
Why can't the medical world find a cure for the common cold?

Roy Lawson
Las Vegas, Nevada

It's far more difficult to cure a viral infection (like the common cold) than a bacterial infection. While bacteria cause trouble merely by living inside the body, viruses go a step further and invade cells, becoming part of them. For this reason, it's easier to kill bacteria without harming the patient.

So vaccination, which stimulates the production of antibodies that prevent a virus from successfully penetrating cells in the first place, is our only recourse. But it's far more complicated to produce a vaccine than it is to simply kill an organism (like bacteria). Then we must multiply this complex vaccination hurdle by a factor of 150 to 200, because there are that many different viruses that cause the symptoms of the common cold. And then, even if we manage to produce that many vaccines, how many of us would even *want* to be vaccinated up to two hundred times? Imagine the problem with side effects alone.

Maybe someday someone will discover an element common to most of those cold viruses, and then there'll be a chance for a successful vaccination (if not a cure). But until that day, it is more likely that we will find a vaccination for AIDS (also caused by a virus) than it is we will defeat the common cold.

Dear Marilyn:
The government turned off our hot-water heater at work to save energy. I say it is not sterile to have to wash your hands in cold water. Some of the women at work say that "it has been proven that hot water does not kill germs—cold water does, and even hospitals use cold water now." So my question is, why do hospitals sterilize instruments with heat?

> Barbara Tipton
> Fort Benning, Georgia

When we wash our hands, we don't sterilize them. With the help of soap and water, we merely mechanically rinse off as many microorganisms as possible. That's because heat sterilization requires far higher temperatures than our hands could ever tolerate—even boiling isn't enough. Other sterilization techniques include irradiation, the use of chemical substances, and filtration. Antiseptics and disinfectants also play an important role. But when we use ordinary tap water, it doesn't make much of a difference whether it's cool, warm, or even hot.

Dear Marilyn:

Would you be willing to estimate, based on probability and scientific evidence, the likelihood that a man would contract AIDS from one unprotected sexual encounter with a woman who is a casual acquaintance, but who appears not to be a prostitute, an IV drug user, or especially promiscuous?

Denny Dow
Hillsboro, Oregon

No; it would lull you into a false sense of security. If everyone based his or her behavior on that number, we would soon be overwhelmed by HIV infection. But I'm willing to tell you that people may be less protected with condoms than they think.

This is because condoms (and condom usage) are far from perfect. However, it's difficult to determine product-failure rates (and usage-failure rates) in the case of pregnancy because failure often results in induced abortion, which is generally underreported. (This appears to be the situation cross-culturally, regardless of whether abortion is legal.) The condoms themselves often fail for several reasons, such as leakage and breakage, and their purchasers often fail to achieve perfection in actual use—real-life conditions, even with careful people, are far less controllable and tidy than those found in laboratories.

In short, condoms are clearly effective products, but are they effective enough to warrant considering them as protection against AIDS infection? No one really knows how well condoms prevent AIDS transmission, but according to the Centers for Disease Control, there was a recent study conducted with monogamous couples, each with one partner testing HIV-positive and the other partner testing HIV-negative. Over a period of two years of what the researchers called "perfect" condom use, not a single HIV-negative partner became HIV-positive. (Other studies have shown a negative-to-positive conversion rate of up to 2 percent.) However, those numbers don't seem to square with the analysis of data (corrected for the underreporting of abortion) from the 1988 National Survey of Family Growth, which reported that 15 percent of women whose partners used condoms became pregnant within a year. Moreover, individual sperm are far larger than any virus, so when we add the consideration of the porosity of the condoms, they should have prevented pregnancy *more* effectively, not *less.*

Statistics are extremely difficult to assess. There could be weaknesses in both sets of studies. For example, in the AIDS study, there might have been comparatively little sexual activity (which would be understandable in this circumstance), or seroconversion (changing from HIV-negative to HIV-positive) might take longer (in incubation) than we think, or just a few false positives and/or false negatives might have ruined the results. ("False positives" are test results that show an uninfected person to be HIV-positive, and "false negatives" are test results that show an infected person to be HIV-negative.)

Another possibility is that a significant number of the uninfected partners may be immune to HIV infection. The phenomenon of immunity to a disease is not rare. Some children don't get chicken pox and some adults don't get the latest influenza, even when clearly exposed. Likewise, it is known that some people get infected with AIDS after a single act of intercourse, and others remain uninfected after years of unprotected intercourse with an HIV-positive partner.

In one important study, couples were chosen because one partner was infected and the other was not. However, this method will self-select every available case of natural immunity into the study group. *Then* the couples were counseled about condom use. But if the uninfected partner had stayed negative *before* using condoms, it's hard to say how much credit to give condoms if this person simply *remains* uninfected. To illustrate the concept, consider the ramifications of initiating a study of the condom as a method of birth control by selecting the next several hundred childless couples who walk by. Every case of male and/or female infertility will thus be included in the study.

It was also noted in this study that the uninfected partner in a relationship of under a year's duration was more likely to convert from negative to positive than one whose relationship was of longer duration. This also suggests that natural immunity may have been playing a role. It could be that all those who *can* become infected *will* become infected within a year or two, and the rest never will. But those dual-infection couples wouldn't have been accepted for the study in the first place.

On the other hand, in the pregnancy studies, some of the women may not have been truthful about their sexual activities. And statistics apart, the study methods themselves can be misleading. For example, it is not uncommon for an IUD (intrauterine device) to "fail" due to expulsion, leading to pregnancy. But in the experience of the women who reported to the two major National Surveys of Family Growth, IUD failure rates were significantly higher than those in any of the clinical trials. (Clinical trials use volunteers who are supposed to follow careful instructions throughout a formal study.) Why the difference? One hypothesis put forward is that the women who reported to the surveys labeled post-expulsion pregnancy as a *failure* of the IUD, whereas women who took part in the clinical trials labeled the occurrence as an *expulsion* of the IUD. Expulsion of an IUD is considered an example of imperfect use, as is slippage of a condom.

Another serious weakness is that the AIDS study was conducted with "perfect" condom use, which means not only using a condom every time, but using it *perfectly* every time. Why is that a weakness? Because when pregnancy studies are done with "perfect" condom use, they, too, conclude that virtually no pregnancy occurs. But in real life, that's not the case at all. Moreover, according to the Centers for Disease Control's *Morbidity and Mortality Weekly Report,* "The determinants of proper condom use are complex and incompletely understood." In short, perfect condom use is not as easy as it seems. (For example, sperm often begins to appear *before* ejaculation.)

For the moment, let's consider the worst case and assume that because condoms are only 85 percent effective in preventing pregnancy (which is commonly thought to be a realistic assessment), they are also only 85 percent effective in preventing AIDS transmission. 85 percent still sounds highly protective. But women are only fertile for a few days a month, and men don't get pregnant at all. Think of the implications with AIDS. Excluding cases of natural immunity, *both* sexes are "fertile" *every* day for AIDS. That is, when condoms are used to prevent AIDS infection transmitted from an HIV-positive partner, their effectiveness plummets when compared to preventing pregnancy. Assuming sexual activity once a day, a failure rate of 15 percent, and an infected partner, a new case of AIDS infection will occur once every *week.* (With weekly activity, a new case will occur every seven weeks; with monthly activity, it will occur every seven months.)

Even if condoms were to become 99 percent effective against AIDS transmission, far beyond what many researchers dare hope, an individual could expect to become infected within three to four months. It's something to think about.

×

Dear Marilyn:

Recently I watched an interesting program about lions and hyenas in Africa, but one segment really disturbed me. A lioness and her three cubs were shown settling into their new den. Soon the mother ventured out in search of food. During her search, she was bitten by a cobra. Ill and disoriented, she wandered around for a week before returning to an empty den. What really disturbed me was that the camera crew did nothing to save the lives of her young. The helpless cubs were filmed starving to death. Eventually, hyenas came and carted off the dead carcasses. Now, I've heard of nature taking its course, but aren't we, as humans, part of nature? Do you think the filmmakers should have come to the aid of the cubs?

Patricia Eng
Bonita, California

I admire your obviously kind heart and good intentions, but we should see this scenario in a broader context than the one you've described. For example, what was the lioness going to get for food? A zebra? Should the camera crew intervene to save the zebra? If they did, what would the lion cubs do for food? And if the lion cubs had survived, what would the hyenas do for food? And if we want the camera crew to be *really* politically correct, we'd insist that they go find the lioness's last mate and make *him* come and take care of the kids.

We're part of nature, all right, but that doesn't mean we should attempt to run it unless we want to turn this planet into a big zoo, instead. Zoos are nice places to visit, but no one wants to live there—including those who do.

Dear Marilyn:

I was disappointed when you upheld the decision of a camera crew photographing starving lion cubs not to intervene. The camera crew could have saved three starving beings. That they remained detached does not speak well for mankind.

Judith Leonard Sabourin
Hudson, Massachusetts

None of us can afford to have your attitude about zoos and intervention if we want an ecosystem where any of us can survive.

Mary Haines

The lion, zebra, and hyenas were capable of taking care of themselves. The cubs were not. This is taking reality too far.

Renée Fineberg Torres
New York, New York

Would you have been able to sit and watch three human babies starve to death? I suspect the camera crew was all male.

Gail Ford
Fairfield, Connecticut

Looking back over my comments, I still believe they make good sense overall. Yes, I'd treat human babies differently, and that unequal treatment makes good sense, too. Otherwise, we'd be stuck rescuing every barnacle that someone scrapes off a boat. Here's one last letter, which I prize.

Dear Marilyn:

Your answer was not only profound, but in thirty years spent in protecting animals, it struck me as one of the few times that such clear and concise advice came from someone outside the animal-protection field. With your obvious understanding of more than just the surface problems that face mankind, I received renewed hope that the humane education that many have spent a lifetime to promote has not been in vain.

With the millions that your column reaches, you have done a far greater good than you could possibly know. On behalf of the staff of the Animal Protection Institute and our 150,000 members throughout the country, you have our gratitude and respect.

Robert Hillman
Vice President of Field Operations
Animal Protection Institute
Sacramento, California

Dear Marilyn:

I've heard that people, like other animals, are strongly attracted to others who they feel possess genetics fit for good offspring. Occasionally, the intensity gets out of hand and turns people to mush. Besides aesthetic and emotional appeal, is there a real definition to "chemistry"?

Torrey Klover
Las Vegas, Nevada

Darned if I know, although I've gotten mushy myself now and then. But whatever it is, I think it's very possibly the finest experience that life has to offer.

Regardless, I disagree with the modern premise that animals are attracted to each other with the well-being of future offspring in mind. Either researchers are trying to endow all creatures with politically correct social behavior, or our graduate schools aren't teaching cause and effect as well as they might. Even a wise old owl doesn't have the foggiest notion that mating may produce little owlets, and he doesn't give a hoot, either. Concluding otherwise is a reversal of cause and effect and is as incorrect as stating that fish developed gills so that they could breathe underwater.

Dear Marilyn:

Of all the creatures known to man, is there any animal other than man that indulges in sex for pleasure rather than for procreation?

Audric Gibson
Paramount, California

Aside from pure instinct, I don't know of any non-human animal that engages in sex for any reason *other* than pleasure. After all, none of them is even intellectually advanced enough to learn how to plant a crop, much less figure out how sex acts relate to baby animals. So if you believe that engaging in sex for pleasure is inherently wrong, you could easily conclude that man is the *most* moral of animals (because he occasionally tries to generate offspring, even if only a couple of times throughout life), rather than the *least* moral of them, as you imply.

Dear Marilyn:

Why is it that photos of ourselves always look a little strange to us? That is, why do we think that everyone *else* looks normal, but we don't think that *we* look "like ourselves"?

Junie Evans
Pittsboro, North Carolina

I have the same feeling myself. It's because photos are the reverse of our mirror image, which is the image *we* see of ourselves. Other people see what the *camera* sees. As an illustration, have a look around the room you're in. Now imagine walking in to see everything reversed—doors, windows, furnishings, and all. Wouldn't that look very strange? That's the feeling of disorientation you get when you look at a photograph of yourself.

Dear Marilyn:

For many people, hearing their voice on tape is a surprising experience. Why is this so?

Reuben Hatch
Salt Lake City, Utah

We're not objective about our own voices because others (including tape recorders) hear them through the air, but we also hear them through our bodies, adding liquid and solid sound transmission, as well. What I wonder is why our voices nearly always seem *worse*. (They're not like photographs that catch us in poses less flattering than those we adopt for the mirror over the sink.) Almost no one thinks, "Oh, is *that* how I sound to others? How nice!"

Dear Marilyn:

How many people were alive at the time of Jesus Christ?

Harvey Stuart
Charlottesville, Virginia

There were about 250 million people, so the density would have been something like spreading out the current population of the United States to cover the entire world instead.

Dear Marilyn:

How many people are there per square land mile in the world?

Henry Zukowski
St. Petersburg, Florida

It's a disquieting figure. With about 5.5 billion people in the world and only 57,160,000 square miles of land, there are about 96 people for every square mile of land to stand on. Without a doubt, it's becoming crowded.

Dear Marilyn:

The fire under Earth's crust is so hot that it melts stone. Where does the fire get the oxygen to stoke it to such intense heat?

Phil Ciaccio
Staten Island, New York

Earth's inner engine doesn't need oxygen. The planet acquired heat during its initial formation as a molten mass, and that heat is supplemented by the decay of radioactive elements, which is a nuclear reaction and not a chemical one that would require oxygen. But hold on to your winter coat, Phil. Despite the fact that the planet still has a great reservoir of heat left, it has been cooling slowly over the years, and our nuclear engine is also running out of fuel. One of these days, even the great volcanoes are going to run out of steam.

Dear Marilyn:

Recently I was in a sailboat in the Gulf of Mexico and was caught in an afternoon thunderstorm. We dropped anchor, battened the hatches, and waited until it passed. Lightning strikes were abundant all around us, but none of them struck the mast, which is fifty-five feet high and made of metal. Why not? It was the tallest object around, and the water was struck several times.

Charles Sull
Tampa, Florida

Contrary to common belief, lightning doesn't always strike the tallest object around. Rather, it will strike the tallest object in a particular bolt's immediate vicinity. That's the reason the misunderstanding is so common—lightning appears to strike tall objects far more often than short ones, which is true. But if a tall object is more than a hundred feet away from a particular lightning bolt, that object won't even be "noticed."

This is also the reason that you're not safe in a storm merely by being shorter than other objects, another popular misconception. If you're standing in an open meadow with nothing else around, not even the Eiffel Tower will protect you if it's a few hundred feet away.

Dear Marilyn:

My companion and I were on a flight from Fort Lauderdale to Phoenix when our plane was struck by lightning. The captain said that in his twenty-three years of flying, he'd never seen anything like it, but we landed safely. Later, we deduced that because a plane isn't grounded, it couldn't be a transmitter of an electrical charge, so it must have struck lightning that was bolting toward the ground, deflecting it off the metal nose cone. With this reasoning, we were grateful that the plane didn't strike the lightning with the wing tip, etc., which isn't rounded enough to deflect it off. Would you please estimate the odds of this occurring?

Sharon Muir
Phoenix, Arizona

They're higher than you might think. An airplane averages one lightning strike per year. Part of the reason this is not so uncommon is that just the presence of the plane itself in the storm appears to trigger a bolt of lightning at times; it intensifies the local electrical field the way a tall metal tower does. (And the body of the plane *does* become part of the lightning path, although usually without harm.)

Dear Marilyn:

Is it true that during a thunderstorm, a car is a safe place to seek refuge? (This area is the "lightning capital" of the nation.) I will be eagerly looking for your answer in the Sunday paper and, in the meantime, hope that I don't get struck by lightning.

Beth Mansbridge
St. Petersburg, Florida

I assume you're still there, Beth, because you were correct about the car being a fairly safe place, all right. If lightning strikes it, as long as you're not in contact with the outer metal frame, it will flash around you and run to ground through the tires. But this is not because rubber is a good conductor of electricity. Actually, rubber is an insulator; it's only because automobile tires contain other conducting materials that they act the way they do.

Dear Marilyn:

If the odds are in favor of something happening—as in a "70 percent chance of rain"—and it doesn't, does that mean that the odds were wrong?

Melanie Plain
San Ramon, California

No. In the rain example, the "70 percent chance" means that out of every 10 days with those atmospheric conditions, the forecaster believes it *will* rain on 7 of those days, and it *won't* rain on *3* of them. The odds would be wrong only if those atmospheric conditions occurred repeatedly, and we discovered that it rained much more or much less often than 7 times out of 10.

Dear Marilyn:

Whenever I hear a weather forecast, and they say there's such-and-such a percentage chance of rain, I become skeptical. Isn't there always a fifty-fifty chance of rain, no matter where you are on Earth? After all, it will either rain, or it won't rain. Since each option is the complete negation of the other, there is no room for any other options, therefore no way that it could be other than fifty-fifty. Is there any way anyone could possibly refute this?

Keith Blackwell
Seattle, Washington

I sure hope so. According to this logic, we can say that either the Sun will come up tomorrow, or it won't. And because there are no other options, the chances are only fifty-fifty that the Sun will come up tomorrow!

But rain doesn't obey the laws of chance in the first place; instead, it obeys the laws of science. It would be far more accurate for a meteorologist to say, "there's a 25 percent chance that a forecast of rain will be correct."

Dear Marilyn:

When viewed from Earth during a solar eclipse, the Moon appears to be exactly the same diameter as the Sun. Is this phenomenon a coincidence, or is there a mathematical reason?

John Farrington
Corning, California

In a way it's a coincidence, but the Moon appears to be of similar size to the Sun all the rest of the time, too. That is, solar eclipses are no exception to that. Take away the drama of the eclipse itself, and the similarity in apparent size seems much less significant.

But the Moon really doesn't appear to be exactly the diameter of the Sun, anyway. It just looks close to that. Depending on when an eclipse occurs, the Moon may even look significantly smaller than the Sun. This is called an "annular eclipse." However, the effect is much less spectacular overall because the brilliant band of full sunlight that surrounds the Moon in that case keeps the sky from darkening.

Moreover, we must travel to a particular location to get the most "coincidental" effect for a total solar eclipse, anyway. Observers outside, but near, the direct path of the eclipse see a partial eclipse instead.

Dear Marilyn:

When a full solar eclipse occurs, isn't it a remarkable coincidence (given the size of and distance between the spheres) that the Moon fits *exactly* in front of the Sun so that only the corona appears?

Bob Connolly
Braintree, Massachusetts

Not really. The only reason we call the event a total solar eclipse is *because* the Moon fits it that way for a brief period of time. The rest of the time, the alignment of the Moon and Sun is much less interesting. For example, an annular eclipse doesn't cause the same darkening of the sky and other total-eclipse phenomena, so most of us Earthlings just don't pay much attention to it.

Dear Marilyn:
Why do astronomers get so excited about viewing the Sun's corona during a total eclipse? Can't they just block out the Sun with a disk over their telescopes any other day?

Donald Gibson
Oakland, California

Not as well as they'd like. A special telescope called a "coronagraph," which blocks out the Sun, is used on a few high mountain sites and space satellites, but the observation effort is fraught with difficulties. The Sun's scattered light must be minimized, the light diffracted (redistributed in intensity) by the telescope must be suppressed, and customized filters and polarization are used, among many other sensitive devices and specialized techniques. Just about everything in science is far more complicated than it looks.

Dear Marilyn:
If day and night are the same length at the vernal and autumnal equinoxes, why aren't sunrise and sunset times the same?

Jill Van Brunt
Succasunna, New Jersey

There are a couple of reasons for this visual discrepancy that people notice. Daylight is actually a few minutes longer on the equinoxes; equal days and nights precede the spring equinox by a few days and follow the fall equinox by a few days. This is because the equinox dates are determined geometrically from the center of the Sun. But in reality, the top of the Sun "rises" into view before its center does.

In addition, the refraction (bending) of the sunlight entering Earth's atmosphere causes some apparent disparity. Like it does at the equator, where days and nights are always equal, this refraction causes the Sun to appear above the horizon "early" at sunrise and to stay "late" at sunset, lengthening the day even more.

Dear Marilyn:

On the longest day in our latitude, I can read a book at 9:00 P.M. But I hear that in Alaska, it remains light much later. How is this so?

J. Robert Rogers
Sacramento, California

North of the equator, we call this the summer solstice, and the reason Alaska gets more daylight is that the North Pole is tilted toward the Sun on that date. At the winter solstice, the South Pole is tilted toward the Sun. This is why the seasons are reversed in the Northern and Southern Hemispheres.

And contrary to popular belief, this tilt of Earth on its axis is what causes the seasons in the first place; they are *not* caused by Earth's distance from the Sun. (Note that winter and summer occur simultaneously in the two hemispheres, so the planet's distance from the Sun can't be significant.) In fact, Earth is farthest from the Sun in the U.S.A.'s summer and nearest to the Sun in our winter. In other words, if Earth weren't tilted, there would be no seasons at all.

But before you move to Alaska to save on your lighting bill, you might be interested to know that every location on the planet, despite the varying hours of daylight over the course of the year, will still accumulate a total of six months of light and six months of darkness.

Dear Marilyn:

We all know that the rise and fall of the ocean tides are caused by the gravitational pull of the Moon as it revolves around Earth. Would this same gravitational pull have any effect on the exact weight of a solid object?

Raymond Stokols
Cliffside Park, New Jersey

Yes. But before you decide to get on the bathroom scale only during high tide, keep in mind that this subject is incredibly complex. The

Moon does indeed attract every particle of Earth, including your body, the air you breathe, and the continent upon which you stand. However, if the Moon attracted every particle equally, there would be no tide at all! It is the minute difference in direction and magnitude of the attractive force (from one point to another) that causes the tidal stress. While their distribution in space and time is known precisely, their overall effect cannot be predicted with current methods.

Dear Marilyn:
    Since there is no "up" or "down" in space, why don't we ever see a falling star fall *up*?

                                        S. Bloom
                                        Huntington Beach, California

Because a meteor (or "falling star") results when a meteoroid enters Earth's atmosphere and either burns up or reaches the surface, when it's then known as a meteorite. (Small ones are termed micrometeorites, but I like to call them "stardust.") This means that an equal number of them fall "up" (or sideways), but we can't see them because the planet beneath our feet is in the way. That is, if Earth were a clear globe, we could look down through Australia and watch meteors falling "up" toward us.

Ten

On Science

"If you put an air mattress and a water bed in the same cool room, you'll sleep just fine on the air mattress, but you'll have to heat the water bed."

Dear Marilyn:

As we know, popcorn pops at different intervals. Why doesn't it just pop simultaneously with one big bang?

Melva Jenkins
Baltimore, Maryland

This is a popular question, but it's a little like asking why leaves don't all fall off trees at the same time. The answer is simply that popcorn kernels are all a little different—like leaves. Then again, maybe it's just Nature's way of going easy on us. Imagine what life would be like, for example, if we were strolling back home from a nice walk and suddenly all the raindrops fell from the clouds at once.

Dear Marilyn:

My husband says that food cooked in a microwave oven cools faster than food cooked in a conventional oven because the faster something heats up, the faster it cools down. Is this true?

Barbara Nadel
Levittown, New York

No. After you remove food from either kind of oven, cooking continues to occur on the inside while the food is cooling on the outside. For this reason, "standing" time is often built into a recipe. But the effect is even *more* pronounced with microwaves than it is with conventional ovens. This is because microwaved food becomes so hot so fast, it must be removed from the oven to prevent the outside from becoming overcooked while the inside is still undercooked. That is, the heat transfer that takes place more leisurely *inside* a conventional oven must take place *outside* a microwave oven, and this lengthens the cooling process. (Microwaves don't penetrate very deeply, so the inside of the food cooks the same way it does in a conventional oven.) In fact, depending on the starting temperature of the food (for example, whether it was frozen) and the temperature of the kitchen, you might find that thirty minutes after you take a roast from your oven, the inside temperature is hotter than it was when you first removed it.

Dear Marilyn:

My sister and I have an ongoing argument. When boiling food, she feels that by turning up the heat, she has reduced the cooking time because the water gets hotter. I maintain that once the water reaches the boiling point, it may boil more furiously, but the temperature remains the same. Who is right, please?

Rosemary Chandler
Sonoma, California

It depends on whether you put a lid on the pot. If not, the water reaches its final temperature once it begins boiling; turning up the heat makes it boil away *faster,* but not *hotter.* If you put a lid on the pot, though, it's a different story. The heavier the lid, the "harder" it is for the water to boil, and the hotter will be the temperature the water can hold. A very tightly capped pot is a version of a pressure cooker, in which the temperature of the water may reach 250°F. In that case, food may take only one minute to cook instead of ten.

On the other hand, you can *decrease* the pressure (instead of *increasing* it with a lid) by taking the pot up to the top of Mount Everest. There, water boils at such a low temperature—around 170°F—that you can boil your vegetables all day without actually cooking them.

Dear Marilyn:

What happens to the wax on a burning candle? I say that it burns. The rest of the family thinks that it evaporates. Please tell me that I'm right as usual.

Ed Olson
Oakland, New Jersey

You're *both* right as usual. The heat of the flame melts the candle-wax fuel and then vaporizes the liquid. The vapor diffuses upward and, at the flame itself, meets oxygen diffusing toward it, where the vapor catches fire and burns. But cheer up, Ed. Burning candles were among the earliest timepieces, and if your conversation had revolved around *that* aspect of them instead, you might get stuck discussing whether the standard definition of the second is the time required for 9,192,631,770 oscillations at the transition frequency of the cesium atom at zero magnetic field *or* the duration of 9,192,631,770 periods of the radiation that corresponds to the transition between the two hyperfine levels of the ground state of the cesium-133 atom. (But at least you'd both be right again.)

Dear Marilyn:

Let's say you have a piece of aluminum in the shape of a doughnut. You heat the doughnut until it is expanding. Does the hole get larger or smaller?

Randy Misener
Belmont, California

It gets larger. The next time you have difficulty opening a glass jar with an aluminum lid, try running warm water over it, and you'll see the principle at work. (The glass expands too, but not as fast.)

Dear Marilyn:

How does a Thermos bottle know when to keep liquids hot or cold?

Frederick Claydon
Northfield, Ohio

Heat travels in the direction of the colder region—whether away from a hot liquid inside the bottle or toward a cold liquid there. And it travels in three different ways—by conduction, convection, and radiation. A typical Thermos bottle blocks those three paths by means of glass liners (to reduce conduction), a near-vacuum space (to reduce convection), and silvering (to reduce radiation). Adding a small neck further creates a "thermal isolation" that will keep heat either from leaving the bottle or from entering it, as the case may be.

Dear Marilyn:

Why does a package of frozen strawberries thaw faster in a bowl of cool water than at room temperature?

Margaret Hushka
Harvest, Alabama

For the same reason that you feel comfortable in a room with a temperature of 72°F, but you feel cold in a pool with that same temperature. Water can "absorb" (actually, conduct) much more heat than air can, and much faster, too. (Roughly, liquids—like water—conduct heat about ten times better than gases—like air—do.) If you put an air mattress and a water bed in the same 72°F room, you'll sleep just fine on the air mattress, but you'll have to heat the water bed, or it'll conduct your body heat away from you, making you feel cold.

Dear Marilyn:
Please settle this dispute. My husband needs the hum of a fan running in order to get a decent night's sleep. In the summer months, this doesn't bother me. However, when the temperatures begin to drop, the cool air is very bothersome. Now for the argument. My husband insists that a fan doesn't lower the temperature. His theory is that the fan simply circulates the temperature already present in a room. I, on the other hand, have pointed out that the sale of fans increases in the warmer months, confirming my belief that fans decrease the temperature in a room. Could you please explain the actual function of the fan and end this nightly bickering? (A romantic dinner is riding on this!)
                    Mrs. D.J.S.
                    Longmeadow, Massachusetts

Fans don't cool the air; they merely circulate it. In fact, electric fans actually *increase* the temperature slightly. (The motor radiates heat, etc.) However, fans *do* cool *you,* mainly by increasing the air circulation over the skin. (You notice the same effect outdoors in winter. That is, you feel colder when the wind blows, even though the temperature remains the same.)

Oddly enough, however, when the temperature climbs too high in the room—say, over one hundred—that same indoor fan can have the opposite effect. By increasing the air circulation over your skin, it makes your sweating more efficient. But sweating requires water, and if you don't drink enough liquid, you can easily become dehydrated, causing body temperature to *rise,* leading to heat exhaustion and possibly death. Every summer, people are found dead from this little-known phenomenon.

Let me know if you still manage to have a romantic dinner after reading this. Wait a minute. If a romantic dinner is riding on this, does it mean that if you win, your husband takes you out for a romantic dinner, and if *he* wins, *you* take *him* out for a romantic dinner? Sounds like a darned good bet!

Dear Marilyn:

Once when I was in China, I commented about how Tibetans would have to get up at five in the morning to make a call to their comrades in Shanghai at eight, as the width of China approximates that of the U.S. But the whole of China has just one time zone. So my wife asked, "If one traveled from Tibet to Shanghai, would one suffer from jet lag?" This would be the equivalent of flying from San Francisco to Boston, and it has been puzzling me ever since. What do you think?

Rodney Takashige
Honolulu, Hawaii

I think that "jet lag" is made far worse by spending the night on the plane, resulting in exhaustion from poor sleep while adjusting to a change in time zones (that is, the sudden change in your sleep/wake schedule), both at once. Let's say that you fly from one end of China to the other in the daytime (so you don't lose sleep). There would be little jet lag, especially if you continue to sleep and wake about the same clock time in your new location, although the difference in sunlight (at the same clock times) might cause some discomfort. Likewise, if New York and London were in the same time zone, and you flew from one to the other the same way, you wouldn't have much jet lag. But when you fly directly north and south—say, from New York to Lima, Peru—there's not jet lag at all.

Dear Marilyn:

When an aircraft breaks the sound barrier, why does it boom just once or twice? That is, why doesn't it boom continuously all along its path?

I hope my "Marilyn" stamp (cut out from your column and pasted on the envelope next to the post-office stamp) got your attention. I think you belong on a stamp more than people like Elvis and Hank Williams.

D. H. Ringer
Virginia Beach, Virginia

The term "breaking the sound barrier" calls an incorrect image to mind. There is no barrier that gets broken like an acrobat jumping through a paper hoop. Subsonic airplanes already generate noise continuously because they produce pressure disturbances (sound) that are transmitted all along their paths, so there are no sudden jolts. But a supersonic aircraft outraces its own pressure disturbance, dragging it along in the shape of a cone instead, one cone from the nose and one from the tail. Whenever we're in the path of those cones racing along the ground, we'll hear a sharp crack (or two) of sound, but mainly because the event is so sudden.

I'll take it as a compliment that you wish I were on a stamp and hope you're unaware that everyone who appears on a stamp is dead. (Of course, in the case of Elvis, some people aren't so sure!)

Dear Marilyn:
Why did kamikaze pilots wear helmets?

Paul O'Hara
Las Vegas, Nevada

They did?! Well, it must have been for the same reason that wealthy old men write out premarital agreements before they marry attractive young women. They both know they're going to go down in flames, but sometimes a false sense of security feels better than none at all!

Dear Marilyn:
Some time ago, a neighbor had problems with her garage-door opener. The door would open for no apparent reason. Eventually it was discovered that when the door opened, an airplane was always flying overhead. The frequency on the opener was changed, and the problem disappeared. Could the reverse be true? That is, can electronic equipment on the ground or in the possession of passengers interfere with the operation of airplanes? On a recent flight, I noticed that the

flight attendant's warning to turn off such equipment was either un-heeded or unheard by several passengers. Are there any serious conse-quences of not following these guidelines?

Michele Simon
West Lawn, Pennsylvania

Electronic equipment on the ground has such a small range that it couldn't affect an airplane unless it were flying right over your rooftop. Such equipment on the plane itself is another matter. Right now, air-lines are unsure about whether devices like radios, disc players, and lap-top computers can affect the operation of the airplane. In the meantime, I think it's irresponsible for any passenger to take a chance. Turning off electronic equipment is more than a guideline—it's an or-der. If you see anyone disregarding it, no matter what the reason, I sug-gest notifying a flight attendant without delay.

Dear Marilyn:

Every time I have helium balloons in my car, I've noticed that they seem to do the opposite of what I expect. While floating in the air, if I accelerate the car, they go *forward*—not backward as everything else in the car does. And if you want them to go to the back of the car, just put on the brakes! I cannot think of any rational explanation for this. Can you?

Pamela Wiebusch
Sarasota, Florida

Helium balloons do the opposite of what we expect even when they're *not* inside a car: because helium is lighter than air, they rise instead of fall. So when a closed car accelerates, and the air trapped inside gets pushed backward, helium balloons move forward. And when a car rounds a curve, helium balloons move into the curve rather than away from it.

Dear Marilyn:

I wonder when I look into the mirror on the passenger's side of my car when I am the driver and see "Warning: Objects in mirror are closer than they appear." Is it because the mirror used on that side is different from the one on the driver's side?

William Kirkland
Mechanicsville, Virginia

Yes; the driver's-side mirror is ordinary. The passenger's is convex (curves outward like a sphere), which allows it to reflect a much wider angle. This has the consequence of distorting the size of the image, but experts believe that the advantage of eliminating the "blind spot" (the place you can't see without turning your head) outweighs the disadvantage.

Dear Marilyn:
    Please settle a discussion on this subject. Which of these is true? "White is the absence of all color, and black is the presence of all color," or "White is the presence of all color, and black is the absence of all color."

Judy Niemann
Homewood, Illinois

There's both incorrect as they stand, but they're both correct if you invert them. Loosely speaking, if you mix all the colors of *light* together, you get "white," but if you mix all the colors of *pigment* together, you get "black." (But just because light is white doesn't mean it contains all the colors of light, and just because pigment is black doesn't mean it contains all the colors of pigment.)

Dear Marilyn:
    On a recent trip, we saw a dry lake bed that ended at the edge of a two-story building. The mirage of water on the lake bed reflected an inverted image of the building. But how can something be reflected in a mirage, which isn't there in the first place?

Alan Thomas
Long Beach, California

Many people think that a mirage is a kind of hallucination seen especially in hot, dry places by people who are almost as hot and dry themselves. But this isn't the case at all—a mirage is an optical illusion, and nothing can appear in a mirage that isn't already around somewhere. Those scenes in movies that show dusty desert travelers looking up to see an oasis with palm trees swaying in the wind are entirely fictional. (Maybe the reason mirages are associated with arid places is that they so often appear to be rippled, almost like water, making them of unusual interest there and arousing false hope.)

There are many different kinds of mirages, depending on atmospheric conditions. In some, an object just out of sight (below the horizon) can appear lifted up into the sky. In others, a portion of the sky can appear down on the ground. And when shimmering in the heat, this can look very much like—as luck would have it—water.

Dear Marilyn:

I have always been under the impression that sailboats could not go any faster than the wind. Yet I recently read an article about a world speed record for sailboats that claimed they could go two to three times as fast as the wind. How is this possible?

E. J. Gerloff III
Virginia Beach, Virginia

Many people understandably believe that the wind is what pushes a sailboat along, and that the difference in sailboat speeds results from how efficiently the boats and their crews manage to capture as much wind as possible. But if that were the case, no one would be able to sail *into* the wind, which they do, even though at an angle.

Not counting the current, the wind is indeed the force applied, but not quite in the way we might imagine. With well-designed sails, it also provides "lift" like an airplane wing. In an airplane with horizontal wings, the lift helps move the plane upward, but in a sailboat with vertical sails, the lift helps moves the boat forward (instead of sideways). This is because the sails are designed to translate sideways wind into forward motion, and the "lift" factor makes that sideways wind just that much more powerful. In fact, the entire craft, hull structure included, turns into a sort of big, wet wing.

Dear Marilyn:

Can you please settle a dispute between my sister and me? Exactly why do ships—or anything, for that matter—float?

Kevin O'Donnell
Worth, Illinois

Any object that floats on (or is submerged in) water is buoyed upward to some extent. This force is caused by the weight of the water it displaces—the water pressure rises higher and higher with increasing depth. And because the object is subject to more pressure from below than from above, it may rise.

The weight of the object is another factor. If it's heavier than the volume of water it displaces, it will sink, and if it's lighter, it will rise. And in anticipation of your next question, yes, if it weighs the same as this volume of water, it will be stationary. This is why a ship floats in place. If it's too light, it'll ride too high in the water and can become unstable enough to roll over; on the other hand, if it's too heavy, it'll ride too low in the water and maybe even sink.

Dear Marilyn:

Some years ago, my husband and I started one of those jar penny collections, to be emptied when full and spent foolishly (actually, for a goat). About a year after we started, one of us deposited two rolls of pennies in the jar, which is a seven-gallon water jar, similar to those atop a water cooler. The rolls were dropped in at approximately an inch or two from the bottom, but despite trying our best to bury them over the years, they seem to keep "floating" to the top. (The jar has about six inches of pennies in it now.) Why does this happen?

Birgit Ayrey
Rocky Hill, New Jersey

The jar is receiving constant tiny shakes throughout the day; over the years, this makes the objects inside it move around the container in a pattern that is dependent both on the shape of the pennies and the shape of the jar. You can demonstrate this phenomenon by filling a cylindrical container with lots of little marbles and one large one, then shaking it until the large one pops up to the surface. But if you take a conical container and fill it with the same marbles, the large one will travel to the bottom, instead.

Dear Marilyn:

If you drop a bullet from one hand, and at the same time you use the other hand (held at the same height) to shoot another bullet straight across an open field, which bullet will hit the ground first, and why?

Chris Comer

Scott Depot, West Virginia

This is a good example of the weakness of our intuition. Most of us would say that the dropped bullet would hit first because it would need to travel only a few feet. But in fact, both bullets will hit the ground at the same time. The sideways force and the downward force don't interfere with each other as they affect the flight of the bullet itself. One force takes the bullet across the field; the other brings it down to earth.

Dear Marilyn:

Aside from the obvious point at the North Pole, where and why are there an infinite number of points on Earth's surface where you can walk a mile south, a mile east, a mile north, and end up at your starting point?

Richard Grant

Farmers Branch, Texas

For one thing, you can start somewhere on a certain latitude circle that is a little more than a mile from the *South* Pole. In that case, given the dimensions of Earth, after you walk a mile south, walking a mile east would take you in exactly one entire revolution around the South Pole, so that walking a mile north would take you right back to your starting point. There would be an infinite number of starting points on that circle.

But for another thing, you might start on a particular latitude circle that is even *closer* to the South Pole, such that after you walk a mile south, walking a mile east would take you in *two* revolutions around it, with the same result. There would be an infinite number of starting points on that circle, too.

Moreover, in addition to the infinite number of starting points on each circle, there would be an infinite number of the circles themselves as you get closer and closer to the South Pole (with a mile away as the limit), revolving around it more and more times.

Dear Marilyn:

Could you please bring the following passage down to earth for us non-scientists? "There simply are limits on what we can know. One of the great discoveries of modern physics is the so-called principle of indeterminacy. According to this insight, when we observe an electron, we can determine its position or its velocity, but we can never know both simultaneously."

R. Guinnan
Rio Rancho, New Mexico

This is known as Heisenberg's "uncertainty principle," and it's one of the more intriguing postulates of a development in modern physics that we call "quantum mechanics." (Together with the theory of relativity, quantum mechanics totally capsized classical physics, which imposes no such limits on observation.)

In short, quantum mechanics describe the behavior of matter and energy on such a small scale that even radiation can be seen as composed of "parts." Specifically, the uncertainty principle states that the process of measurement in itself disturbs whatever is being measured. For example, if we attempt to measure the position of an atom by viewing it, the necessary light interacts with that atom, imparting a change. This has philosophical implications, too. In the above example, what if the light was already there? Should we subtract all influences? And would subtracting all influences leave nothing at all?

Dear Marilyn:

My science teacher says that two objects can't occupy the same space at the same time. I disagree with her, and I told her I would prove that two objects *can* occupy the same space at the same time. So I was wondering if you could help me. I'd appreciate it a lot! Thanks.

Kerri Nigita
Easton, Pennsylvania

No problem. For a good proof, just take your science teacher on the subway in New York City at rush hour.

Eleven

On Thinking Analytically

"Think of mental exercise
like physical exercise."

Dear Marilyn:

In your responses to questions, the logic of your explanations make it appear so effortless. Do you think that problem-solving and critical-thinking skills can be learned and developed? If so, how?

Stephanie Zinger
Howard Beach, New York

I'm confident they can be learned, and the key is having the right attitude. Think of mental exercise like physical exercise. If you do only as much physical exercise as you need to accomplish your day-to-day tasks, you'll soon find yourself incapable of doing anything more. And any little bit of exertion that you save—like driving around the department-store parking lot to find the parking space that's closest to one of the doors—narrows your physical world just that much more. If you operate only within your comfort zone, not only do you not expand it, your comfort zone quietly shrinks. I was at a concert hall last week and watched at least a hundred people line up at the escalator to ride up the equivalent of two sets of stairs. A broad marble staircase was right next to the escalator. There were fewer than half a dozen people on it.

It's the same way with mental exercise. Every day you must press yourself to do a little more than you can do easily. Play games that make you think, not games of chance. Read a book that's a bit difficult for you. Take a course in any academic subject. Will this make you feel dumb at first? Yes. It's just like the feeling you get when you go to the gym for the first time. You feel out of breath and out of shape. And you are! But with time, all the old abilities will come back, and you'll feel just great. Try it!

Dear Marilyn:

Why does the public equate high intelligence with the ability to work with numbers?

K. Faye Angle
Tampa, Florida

Probably because it's a conclusive way to prove reasoning power. Math answers are the ultimate in objectivity: they're either right or wrong, with very little in between. (Advanced mathematics is not involved, though. If you don't know anything about the determination of minima, maxima, and inflexions, it means absolutely *nothing* except that you haven't studied differential calculus.)

Dear Marilyn:

I am impressed by your mathematical ability. I have a high grade-point average in college, but I know this will go down when I take algebra. I simply cannot get algebra through my head. Do you have any advice for me?

Cindy Gredesky
Woodbury, New Jersey

Yes, but you may not like it. You should go back and buy an introductory high-school algebra text and work through it from the beginning. (Be sure to obtain the most elementary one you can find.) I also suggest that you reason through the problems in addition to using the formulae. This reasoning process is crucial to later mathematical thinking, and if you don't learn it early, you may never learn it at all.

Yours is a common problem, and I have my own theory about why so many people have difficulty with mathematics: Most people don't have a tendency to perfectionism (thank goodness for them), but the study of mathematics requires it. Every step of the way, strict attention to the smallest detail is absolutely necessary. If you can learn to acquire the trait of perfectionism for certain courses, you'll succeed much more easily at math.

Dear Marilyn:

Who invented algebra and geometry? I'm a student, and I believe that neither one of them will be of any use in life! Do I *really* have to know the geometric mean between two numbers in any job I will be in? The person who invented them must have been really bored!

Barbra Tolentino
Sarasota, Florida

Algebra and geometry go back to the very beginning of civilization and are found in the first written records of humankind, including ancient cuneiform (the characters used in Sumerian, Akkadian, Assyrian, and Babylonian writing). In fact, what later came to be known as the Pythagorean theorem (which states that the sum of the squares of the two sides of a right triangle is equal to the square of the hypotenuse) appears on clay tablets that date from the third millennium B.C.

But on behalf of parents and math teachers all across the nation, I think the common complaint about mathematics not being useful later in life is just an excuse for not wanting to work harder than is necessary. Do you think you shouldn't study the U.S. Constitution because you'll never again need to be able to recite the Bill of Rights? Do you think you shouldn't participate in physical education because you'll never again need to be able to do a sit-up? Of course not. Both of these subjects (and many more) are part of the broad education that is essential for us all to raise ourselves out of ignorance and become assets to both ourselves and our country. And if you study enough mathematics, your logical abilities will improve, and you won't continue to make such bad excuses!

Dear Marilyn:

Is there any practical use for algebra outside of careers directly related to math and science? I plan on being a journalist. Will I ever need to use algebra in my everyday life on the job?

Lisa Bintrim
New Freedom, Pennsylvania

I sympathize, but we all need as many math courses as we can stand because they teach us how to think logically and how to reason through problems in all areas of our lives, not just the more number-related ones. (And by the way, if a journalist can't cope with algebra, how is she going to cope with things like misleading statistics and economic plans and business trends?)

Dear Marilyn:

My young son brought home the following math problem as part of his homework: "Ben decides to use a new pattern for building trains. He uses 1 block for his first train, 3 blocks for the second, and 6 blocks for the third. How many blocks will he need for the sixth train? Think! Look for a pattern!" I gave him an answer of 15, and it was wrong according to the teacher. I used a 1, 3, 6, 9, 12, 15 pattern. Does this problem have only one correct answer, or can there be more than one depending on how you make your pattern?

Ginni Maxwell
Alexandria, Virginia

This is an important issue in testing overall. In sum, if a problem has more than one answer—*and those answers are all equally good*—the problem itself is not good. In the case of a good problem, arguments typically arise when people assume that all answers are equally good as long as they're not clearly wrong. But that is not the case—either in testing or in life—and this mistaken belief accounts for many scores that otherwise would be higher.

Your own answer happens to be incorrect. If it patterned additions of 3, the series would have to start with 0 for the pattern to follow with 3, 6, 9, 12, 15; because the series starts with 1, the pattern would have to follow with 4, 7, 10, 13, 16. A correct answer to the problem is 21 blocks: Ben starts with nothing. For train #1, he adds 1 block (to zero) and makes train #1 out of 1 block. For train #2, he adds 2 blocks (to train #1's 1 block) and makes train #2 out of 3 blocks. For train #3, he adds 3 blocks (to train #2's 3 blocks) and makes train #3 out of 6 blocks. For train #4 he adds 4 blocks (to train #3's 6 blocks) and makes train #4 out of 10 blocks. For train #5, he adds 5 blocks (to train #4's 10 blocks) and makes train #5 out of 15 blocks. For train #6, he adds 6 blocks (to train #5's 15 blocks) and makes train #6 out of 21 blocks. Here's the pattern: 1, 3, 6, 10, 15, 21. (To zero, we added 1, then 2, then 3, then 4, then 5, and then 6.)

But the problem started with only 1, 3, and 6. A person could argue that the series can be based on prime numbers (numbers greater than 1 that can be divided only by themselves and 1), making the next number 11 instead of 10. We start with 1, the first number in the series. To that first number 1, we add 2—the first prime—to get 3, the second number in the series. To that second number 3, we add 3—the second prime—to get 6, the third number in the series. To that third number 6, we add 5—the third prime—to get 11 as the fourth number in the series. To that fourth number 11, we add 7—the fourth prime—to get 18 as the fifth number in the series. To that fifth number 18, we add 11—the fifth prime—to get 29 as the sixth number in the series. So Ben would need 29 blocks, not 21. Here's the pattern: 1, 3, 6, 11, 18, 29. (To 1, we added 2, then 3, then 5, then 7, and then 11.)

Both answers stand to reason. Which is better? This is a good exercise for "thinking" debate, including not just mathematics, but philosophy and psychology, as well. I believe the first of the two answers is better. What do *you* think?

Dear Marilyn:

Please help settle a dispute. Two people are each asked by a third person to guess a number from 1 through 10. Whoever gets closer to the number chosen by the third person wins. Does the first or second guesser have the advantage?

Anonymous
Norman, Oklahoma

Let's say that the first person chooses randomly, the second person chooses knowledgeably, and the winner gets to throw a whiffle ball at the loser. In this case, the second person will win most of the time. Say that Tom chooses 1; Roseanne should choose 2 to win 9 times out of 10. If he chooses 2, she chooses 3 to win 8 times out of 10; if he chooses 3, she chooses 4 to win 7 times out of 10. And if he chooses 4, she chooses 5 to win 6 times out of 10. The same works when Tom chooses 7, 8, 9, and 10, in which cases Roseanne chooses 6, 7, 8, and 9 respectively. Only if he chooses 5 or 6 does she not have an advantage.

Let's say that Tom catches on and chooses either 5 or 6, which means that Roseanne chooses 6 or 5 respectively to maximize her chances. But because these are the only two cases that don't give a knowledgeable second person an advantage, those chances are merely even. That is, they can bean each other back and forth forever, but neither will come out ahead in the long run.

Dear Marilyn:

A friend invited me to walk a one-mile race with her. She walked in the first lane and I in the second. Starting and finish lines were the same. We rounded fourteen corners, and at every corner she got ahead of me, but I always caught up with her on the long stretches. We walked as fast as we could. She finished one step ahead of me and got the gold medal. They clocked me a second behind her, and I got the silver. When we parted, she said, "I wish we both could have had the gold medal." "Yes," I said, "I walked farther than you." She said, "But you have longer legs." What do you think?

Barbara Hollister
Dillsboro, North Carolina

I think the starting lines should have been staggered to compensate for so many turns, which would have made you the winner. The length of your legs isn't grounds for consideration. No one complains that a basketball player's performance should be discounted because he's taller than the others. Physical traits and performance—whether natural or developed—are the essence of competitive sports.

Dear Marilyn:
  Let's say there are five cars on display as prizes, and their five ignition keys are in a box. You get to pick one key out of the box and try it in the ignition of one car. If it fits, you win the car. What are your chances of winning a car?

John Weaverly
Madison, Wisconsin

There's a temptation to say 1 out of 25, but the chances are actually much better than that—1 out of 5. That's because any ignition key is a working key, so they all have equal value. You then need only choose the matching car out of five.
  But if you'd asked the chances of winning any *particular* car—say, the red one that an audience member likes—the answer would be only 1 out of 25. That's because you'd have 1 out of 5 chances of choosing the right ("red") key in the first place, and then you'd still have to choose the right (red) car.
  But if *you* (the contestant) have the red one in mind, your chances would go back up to 1 out of 5. That's because you'd simply take any key and walk right over to the red car. If it fits, you'd win, and with only five keys to choose from, the chances of that happening are 1 out of 5.

Dear Marilyn:

It is my contention that speeding on the interstate highway is not dangerous. Is there any evidence that those who regularly speed have a higher incidence of accidents? I believe other behavior really causes accidents—like unsafe lane changes, poor use of brakes, and tailgating. If I'm correct, what is the purpose of ticketing speeders, other than generating revenue?

C.A.

Fargo, North Dakota

The answer lends itself nicely to misinterpretation, so let's employ this as an example of how to use good statistics to reach bad conclusions, which has become epidemic these days. According to the National Highway Traffic and Safety Administration, the following percentages show the relative speed involved in automobile accidents in 1992. (Figures are rounded to the nearest percent; "unknown" was less than 1 percent)

20 mph or less	2%
25 or 30 mph	29%
35 or 40 mph	31%
45 or 50 mph	17%
55 mph	19%
60 to 65 mph	2%

We can look at the above figures and arrive at the (flawed) conclusion that it must be relatively safe to speed because so few accidents are recorded at high speeds. But this ignores the fact that speed limits are a fact of modern life, so many (if not most) accidents don't occur at high speeds because drivers are so often observing the law when they have an accident. (Note the cluster around 30 miles per hour, a common local speed limit, and the drop in accident rates after 55 miles per hour, a common speed limit on interstate highways.) That is, those figures might amount to nothing more than a chart of average driving speed, interrupted and recorded only because an accident occurred.

It would also be erroneous to assume that people who speed don't also change lanes unsafely, use their brakes poorly, and tailgate, or even that *you* don't make mistakes that cause collisions. After all, that's why we call them "accidents."

And even if we manage to isolate speed as a factor, there are physical limitations to all roads, which is an important factor in determining the speed limit. That is, unless roads are designed and built with higher speed in mind, taking such things as entries and exits, steepness of grade, and bridges into consideration, those higher speeds are unsafe for those roads.

And I'll leave you with one final thought. Envision someone *else* (speeder or not) braking too hard in front of you, or just having your tire blow out at 50 miles per hour; now envision it occurring at 80 miles per hour. The difference is clear. In other words, speeding may be fine if nothing goes wrong, but we can say the same thing about bungee-jumping, demolition derbies, and wing-walking.

Dear Marilyn:

I'm having a problem with the figures in the illustration below, which was captioned, "Men consume about 76 percent of all alcoholic beverages. Percentage consumed:"

I see it as follows: of people who drink, 76 percent are men, and 24 percent are women. But according to the illustration of alcohol consumed, 57 percent is by men, and 43 percent is by women. Help!

K.B.

Highland, Indiana

This is a good example of why statistics are confounding. Assuming all the figures cited are accurate, your first statement ("Of people who drink . . .") is unjustified; the caption instead tells us that 76 percent of alcohol is consumed by men. That's different.

Your second statement (". . . of alcohol consumed . . .") is incorrect; the illustration only shows the percentages by beverage categories. This is misleading because the equal size of the bottles implies that the four categories are sold in equal amounts, but they're not. If much more beer and liquor are sold than wine and wine coolers, the caption can still be correct.

Dear Marilyn:

If my two roommates and I are going to share a giant pizza equally, how do we cut it so that we're all really sure that we've gotten the same amount? The problem is that the pizza is round, but let's say we have a yardstick handy.

Bob Rule
Eustis, Florida

Any one of you takes the yardstick and begins to pass it over the whole pizza (from crust to crust) very slowly so that it continues to define a larger and larger piece. As soon as anyone (including the one with the yardstick) believes that this piece is equal to a third, that person says, "Stop." He cuts off the piece and gets it for himself as he's clearly satisfied this is a fair share. The remaining two must think he's gotten a little *less* than a third, or one of *them* would have said, "Stop."

One of those two people now cuts the remainder into two pieces in such a way that he would be satisfied with either of them. Then the other person chooses one for himself. As that other person thought these two pieces together comprised at least two-thirds of the pizza, he'll be satisfied by getting to choose between them, picking whichever he thinks is a little larger, or either one if he thinks they're the same. The person with the knife will be satisfied with the last piece because he's the one who cut the remainder in what he believed was an equal way.

And I'll bet you thought you were going to get stuck with geometry in this answer, didn't you?

Dear Marilyn:

It drives me nuts when I see the post–holiday season sale prices, especially on clothes. It amazes me that they have that much of a markup the rest of the time, and it makes me feel like such a fool for ever paying the full price! Maybe I just want to make myself feel better, but am I missing something?

June Wiest
San Diego, California

Yes, those sales prices are great bargains. Many people believe that if a tie first sells for $50, then gets reduced to $35, and finally goes down to $20 if it still hasn't sold, the store must have paid far less than $20 for it in the first place (or they wouldn't sell it for $20). But what would be the store's alternative? Even if the store paid $40 for the tie, it would be better to sell it for $20 than to discard it, which would add $0 to their bank account.

Let's say that a store's tie-buyer underestimates the customers' taste and buys fifty ties with little smiley-faces painted on them for $40 each, pricing them at $50 each. By the end of the holiday season, forty-nine ties are left unsold. (One was sold to a woman who couldn't stand her husband.) Dismayed, the store reduces the price to $25 each to get rid of the darned things. (So far, the store has spent $2,000 and taken in $50.) At the end of the sale season, forty-eight ties are left unsold. (Another one was sold to a woman who couldn't stand her son-in-law.) After transferring the buyer to the children's department, the store reduces the price to $10 each. (The store has now spent $2,000 and taken in $75.) At this point, someone like you walks in, picks up one of the ties, and says, "The *nerve* of these people. They must be making a *fortune* in this place. No *wonder* they've got Newt Gingrich's face painted on all these ties."

Dear Marilyn:

Let's say that we decide to dispense with men entirely and boost the number of women in the country. All women would get together and agree to the following. As soon as a woman gives birth to a boy, she would have no more children. But as long as she gives birth to a girl, she can have another child. This way, no family would have more than one boy, but plenty of families would have several girls. Do you see anything wrong with this?

Anonymous
Cupertino, California

Yes! Also, it wouldn't work. Let's say that 64 women give birth, half to boys and half to girls. The half with boys end their families. (There are now 32 boys and 32 girls.) The half with girls (32) give birth again, half to boys and half to girls. (This adds 16 boys and 16 girls, so there are now 48 boys and 48 girls.) The half with boys stop, and the half with girls (16) give birth again, half to boys and half to girls. (This adds 8 boys and 8 girls, so there are now 56 boys and 56 girls.) The half with boys stop, and the half with girls (8) give birth again, half to boys and half to girls. (This adds 4 boys and 4 girls, so there are now 60 boys and 60 girls.) The half with boys stop, and the half with girls (4) give birth again, so there are now 62 boys and 62 girls.) The half with boys stop, and the half with girls (2) give birth again, one to a boy and one to a girl. (This adds 1 boy and 1 girl, so there are now 63 boys and 63 girls.) The one with a boy ends her family, and the one with a girl, after proclaiming herself the unluckiest woman in the country, enters a convent.

Dear Marilyn:

Suppose that you intend to have four children. There are three possibilities: they may all be of one sex, or there may be three of one sex and one of the other, or the sexes may be balanced two and two. Which possibility is most likely?

Adrian Beck
Joplin, Missouri

I know this sounds strange, but more families with four children have three of one sex and one of the other than any other combination. The chances of having all girls or all boys are 1 out of 8, the chances of having two girls and two boys are 3 out of 8, and the chances of having three girls (or three boys) and one boy (or one girl) are 4 out of 8.

Dear Marilyn:

The money at stake is minimal, but a bet has been placed on this question. You have been selected as the objective referee. A man makes the following claim. "I have four children. At least one of these children is a boy. What is the probability that I have exactly two boys and two girls?" Assuming that a boy or a girl is equally likely as an individual event, one of us claims that the chance is 37.5 percent that the man has two boys and two girls. The other of us says that since boys and girls are equally likely, the chance is 50 percent that the man has two boys and two girls. I know I am correct, but we need to see it from another source before one of us will accept my guess. What is your answer?

Tim Riener
Fremont, California

I hope there are three of you because two of you are wrong. The answer is 40 percent. If the man has four children, here are the possible boy/girl combinations.

1) BBBB	5) BGBB	9) GBBB	13) GGBB
2) BBBG	6) BGBG	10) GBBG	14) GGBG
3) BBGB	7) BGGB	11) GBGB	15) GGGB
4) BBGG	8) BGGG	12) GBGG	16) GGGG

The first 15 of those combinations contain at least one boy. (No. 16 has only girls.) Of those first 15, 6 contain exactly two boys and two girls (Nos. 4, 6, 7, 10, 11, and 13.) So the chances of the man having two boys and two girls are 6 out of 15, or 40 percent.

Dear Marilyn:

Many of us have seen the report of the University of Chicago's "National Health and Social Life Survey" stating that "The typical male has about six partners over his lifetime, and the typical female has two." Assuming the typical male is heterosexual, and since the number of males and females is approximately equal, is there any statistical possibility of there being any truth in this survey?

R. F. Yonash
Graton, California

Yes, there is. You've assumed the word "typical" means "average," which most people take to refer to the arithmetical average of the numbers. But "average" also means "middle" and "most common." (Statisticians call these three kinds of averages the "mean," the "median," and the "mode," respectively.) Say you're going to have five guests of the following ages at your next formal dinner party: 100, 99, 17, 2, and 2. (You invited two dozen people in all, but because you're a statistician, most refused to come.)

You inform the butler that the average age of your guests is 44 (100+99+17+2+2=220÷5=44), and he heads downstairs. Just to be on the safe side, you inform the footman that the average age of your guests is 17 (the age right in the middle), and he heads upstairs. And to make *sure* everything is right, you inform the cook that the average age is 2 (the most common age), and he heads to the kitchen. Voilà! It's

8:00, and everyone is treated to puréed peas accompanied by Michael Jackson's latest compact disc, followed by a truly fine cognac afterward. (And you wonder why people are always "out of town" when you have a dinner party.)

In the case of the sex survey, "typical" may well have referred to "most common," which would fit right in with all the old stereotypes. (That is, if you believe sex surveys.)

Dear Marilyn:

I have just read an article that states that of Americans over 85, four of five women, and two of five men, have outlived their spouses. Isn't one a function of the other? How can there be two different statistics? One indicates 80 percent of women over 85 have lost their spouses; the other says 60 percent.

> Ed Gilroy
> Columbia, South Carolina

Not everyone has been married, of course, but the statistic works mathematically even if they have. Consider this case. Suppose there are only ten people over 85 in a statistically perfect town, five of them women and five of them men. One of the women has a living husband, and three of the men have living wives. That one woman's husband may be under 85, but if he isn't, he's one of the three men who have living wives. And the other two men would have wives under 85. Or suppose there are twenty older people in the town, fifteen of them women and five of them men. Three of the women have living husbands, and three of the men have living wives. But even if none of the three women's husbands are under 85, that just means that the three women's husbands are those three men with living wives.

Dear Marilyn:

Suppose a person was having two surgeries performed at the same time. If the chances of success for surgery "A" are 85 percent, and the chances of success for surgery "B" are 90 percent, what are the chances that both will fail?

> Shelly S.
> Silver Spring, Maryland

Assuming the surgeries are completely independent of each other, the chances that both will fail are only 1.5 percent, and the chances that both will succeed are 76.5 percent. (Also, the chances that A will succeed, but B will fail are 8.5 percent; the chances that B will succeed, but A will fail are 13.5 percent.)

Dear Marilyn:

Everyone at work has been arguing about this, and we decided to ask you to settle it. There were three main candidates in the presidential election of 1992. Regardless of the electoral college, suppose the popular vote had gone like this: Say that a majority of the voters preferred Bill Clinton to George Bush, and a majority of the voters preferred George Bush to Ross Perot. Would this have meant that a majority of the voters preferred Bill Clinton to Ross Perot?

William Hoynne
Tempe, Arizona

No. In addition—and this is astounding news for most of us—it even could have easily meant that a majority of the voters actually preferred *Ross Perot* to *Bill Clinton*. Here's how it could have happened. Let's say that one-third of the voters ranked Clinton as No. 1, Bush as No. 2, and Perot as No. 3, and that another one-third of the voters ranked Bush as No. 1, Perot as No. 2, and Clinton as No. 3, and that another one-third of the voters ranked Perot as No. 1, Clinton as No. 2, and Bush as No. 3.

		#1	#2	#3
A)	⅓ ranked	Clinton	Bush	Perot
B)	⅓ ranked	Bush	Perot	Clinton
C)	⅓ ranked	Perot	Clinton	Bush

Looking back at that chart, you can see that even if a two-thirds majority of the voters (A and C) preferred Clinton to Bush, and a two-thirds majority of the voters (A and B) preferred Bush to Perot, a two-thirds majority of the voters (B and C) preferred Perot to Clinton!

Dear Marilyn:

Much has been said about Bill Clinton's alleged draft dodging, with implications of self-interest at best and cowardice at worst. Politics aside, I have had reservations about the reasoning involved and have tried to evaluate the question logically. Here are my points. About 8,744,000 people served in the Vietnam War; there were 47,369 deaths in battle. Forty-one people have served as President; 4 were assassinated in office. Therefore, the chances of being killed in Vietnam were about 1 in 185; the chances of being killed while in office were about 1 in 10. Am I correct in suggesting that the presidency is by far the more potentially dangerous position?

Charlene Robbins
Paragould, Arkansas

Well, that's a novel way to look at it, all right! But numbers are inadequate to describe personal attributes such as courage. In this case, for example, they fail to take risk versus reward into consideration. That is, you attached numbers to the risk, but you didn't attach them to the reward.

Few of us would be willing to bet $1 for a fifty-fifty chance of winning an additional penny. But we'd all bet $1 for a fifty-fifty chance of winning $1 billion. The risks are equal, but the rewards are vastly different.

As the risks and rewards fluctuate, so does human behavior. Envision carrying a heavy pack through a rice paddy as the penny reward (in this case, the reward falls through the floor and has about as much appeal as a punishment); now envision being the leader of the Free World as the $1 billion reward (and in this case, the reward soars through the roof). Now say that your bet for the latter would have to go up to $100. Or that your chances would decrease to only 1 in 3. You'd still want to take that bet. That's the effect of risk versus reward.

Numbers are an excellent aid to reasoning, but it's an increasingly common error to use only the numbers we have available and fail to quantify the rest of the situation. (We may as well ask why anyone would spend millions of dollars running for the presidency when the salary is only $200,000 a year!) As a result, we not only make errors—we may miss the point entirely.

Dear Marilyn:

While exploring math during a college course, I came across something called "Aristotle's Wheel Paradox." As the larger wheel rolls from A to B, the smaller wheel rolls from C to D. If the larger wheel rolls without slipping, there is, at any given time, a point on the perimeter of the large wheel touching the line AB, and at the same time, there is a point on the perimeter of the small wheel touching the line CD. So every point on the large wheel can be correlated with every point on the small wheel. Doesn't this prove that the two perimeters are the same length? But it's obvious that they aren't. How do you account for it?

James Beeman
Auburn, Washington

I don't think this is an answer you're going to want to hear! The resolution of this apparent paradox lies with the concept of densities of infinities and the correspondingly unique qualities of transfinite numbers; the number of points on any segment of a curve is described by the second of the transfinite numbers, known as aleph-one. (Don't complain. I warned you, didn't I?)

Dear Marilyn:

All of the people to whom I have written, some of whom are frequently able to provide clarification on highly arcane subjects, have drawn a blank on one of the commonest mysteries confronting people who use parking meters. Parking meters often have a notice to the effect that "Police will not turn handle." What dire consequences result when a law-enforcement officer turns the handle? Who really cares who turns the handle? If the meter user is a law-enforcement officer, does he or she ask someone else to turn the handle? Is this prohibition intended to redirect police effort from handle-turning to watching for law violations? Is handle-turning by police an underreported crime? In

short, what is the purpose of the notice concerning officers' not turning the handle of a parking meter?

James Wachob
Chevy Chase, Maryland

The purpose is to prevent you from getting away with putting a coin
in the slot, not turning the handle, and removing the coin when you
return to your car. (Please stop blushing, James. We all have days like
this.)

Twelve

On Games, Gaming, and Gambling

"Mary, if I knew how to answer
your question, we wouldn't need
lotteries anymore."

Dear Marilyn:

How would you define a "perfect game" in baseball? Currently, it's defined as a game of at least nine innings in which a pitcher allows no hits, and no opposing player reaches a base in any other way. However, shouldn't it be defined in terms of absolute perfection, instead? Two examples seem obvious:

(A) The pitcher strikes out twenty-seven batters on eighty-one pitches.

(B) The pitcher retires twenty-seven batters on twenty-seven pitches, by groundouts or fly balls, including foul-ball pop-ups.

I would argue that (B) should constitute the perfect game because it achieves the maximum amount of a pitcher's efficiency with the minimum amount of effort. I would also argue that a perfect game has never been achieved. What do you think? We baseball fans would be interested in your opinion.

John Boyd
Silver City, New Mexico

I think it would serve those guys right if we were to threaten to redefine the perfect game the next time they're away on strike! But I don't find good justification to support either one of your examples. Game A would only define the perfect pitcher—the rest of the fielders might just as well be asleep. Game B would only define the perfect fielding— a pitcher whose first pitch gets batted every time is far from perfect! So the current "perfect game" seems like a good compromise.

But—the folks at the National Baseball Hall of Fame in Cooperstown, New York, don't agree with me. They insist that a "perfect game" has little to do with the other fielders and that it describes only a perfect *pitcher*—in which case, you'd think they'd define it as Game A, wouldn't you?

Dear Marilyn:

With respect to how one would define a perfect game in baseball, you said that instead of a nine-inning (or more) game in which a pitcher allows no hits, and no opposing player reaches a base in any other way, a perfect pitcher would be defined by striking out twenty-seven batters on eighty-one pitches. That's not specific enough. I submit that each strike of the eighty-one pitches thrown must be a swinging strike. If any pitch is called a strike, it may be attributable not to the pitcher's perfection, but rather to a missed call by the umpire or an erroneous judgment of the pitch by the hitter.

Patrick Sullivan, Judge
Court of Appeals of Indiana
Indianapolis, Indiana

Hmmm. But a swinging strike might *also* be due to erroneous judgment of the pitch by the hitter. Then again, maybe a pitcher who gets batters to swing—regardless of the ball—can be called a good pitcher. I don't know. But I do think we should stop here, Judge, or eventually we're going to get stuck with the question, "What would happen if the perfect pitcher faced the perfect batter?"

Dear Marilyn:
    In baseball, which pitch can be hit farther—a slow ball or a fastball? I maintain that a slow ball can be hit farther because the bat has less force to overcome when reversing the direction of the pitched ball and so has more energy to accelerate the ball. My detractors at work maintain that it is common knowledge that a fastball can be hit farther. Please let us have your opinion with corroborating evidence, if possible.

Jack Levantino
Phoenix, Arizona

It seems to go against reason, but a fastball can be hit farther than a slow ball because a fastball's own energy is used in its flight back off the bat and toward the outfield. To convince yourself, just toss a tennis ball lightly against a wall; it bounces back lightly. Then throw it harder against the wall; it bounces back harder. If the wall had to absorb all the energy from the ball first, neither ball would then bounce back; they'd just slide down to the ground.

Dear Marilyn:
    Please solve a long-standing question between me and my sons. Does a baseball thrown by a pitcher really curve, swerve, etc.? I have heard that the "curve" is merely an illusion caused by seams or stitches on the ball cover.

Russell Forrest
Carnegie, Pennsylvania

Balls do curve, hop (as with a so-called "rising" fastball), and rotate (as with a knuckleball) due to asymmetric and/or differential forces. The seams play a part in the knuckleball, but it's not an optical illusion; the thrown ball, which doesn't rotate, is actually diverted by the difference in drag caused by stitches in one place and smooth faces in others. And a curveball actually curves, stitches or not.

Dear Marilyn:

I am a widow retiree who plays cards. In our regular pinochle games, I always seem to get less than my share of aces, and one of the other ladies always seems to get more than her share. It makes me so discouraged I feel like quitting. My college-professor son says he doubts I really get significantly fewer aces "over the long haul." In short, he doesn't believe I can have consistently bad luck on the deal. What do you say?

Frances Balfour
Port Richey, Florida

I do believe you could have *had* bad luck, but that doesn't mean you should quit. Regardless of how many (or how few!) aces you've been dealt in the past, your chances of aces in the future are the same as anyone else's chances.

Dear Marilyn:

When I play in card games, I like to shuffle the cards several times, but I'm often told that if I shuffle them too much, they'll be returned to their original order. What are the odds of this happening with five to ten shuffles?

Teri Hitt
Irving, Texas

You aren't a magician, are you? A study shows that with ordinary imperfect shuffles, you need at least seven to make sure that the cards are randomly mixed. Six aren't quite enough, but eight aren't a significant improvement, although the mixing does improve with each shuffle. However, some magicians are so deft with their hands that they can shuffle the cards "perfectly," meaning a shuffle in which the deck is exactly halved, and every single card is interwoven back and forth (with the bottom card prior to the shuffle remaining the bottom card after the shuffle). If you instead do *this* eight times, the cards will be returned to their original position before the shuffling began!

✖

Dear Marilyn:

What are odds, and how are they determined? That is, if the odds in a horserace are 1:1, is this the same as a fifty-fifty chance of heads or tails when you flip a coin? Does it mean a horse has an even chance of either winning or losing?

Cheryl Menninger Wray
Hastings, Nebraska

There is great confusion about this subject. Mathematical chances and mathematical odds are related, but they're different concepts. "Chances" describe the probability of a particular event occurring when other events are equally likely. In the random flip of a coin, the chances of getting heads are 1 out of 2. This is written as ½ (or, after carrying out the division, 50 percent). On the other hand, "odds" describe the probability of an event occurring versus the probability of it *not* occurring. In the coin example, the odds of getting heads are 1 to 1. This is written as 1:1.

But horse racing isn't a matter of chance. That is, a horse will not be chosen as the winner at random. Instead, race results are dependent on the performance of the horse, the jockey, track conditions, and the like. So your question actually refers to pari-mutuel betting, a system of mutual wagering that is related to mathematical odds, but is yet *another* different concept.

In it, the money bet on the horses is placed in a pool. (There are several kinds of bets, so there are several pools.) The pari-mutuel odds on each horse are then calculated to reflect the potential payoff, *not* the mathematical chances or mathematical odds of that particular horse winning. That is, the pari-mutuel odds are only a reflection of what the bettors think, which is what determines the payoff (after subtracting a percentage for the racetrack and for the government). And to complicate the matter even further, most gambling odds are expressed as the odds *against* winning. In other words, when a horse is "10 to 1," most bettors think it won't win, but if it does, that horse will pay back $10 (plus your $1 bet) for every $1 bet on it.

Dear Marilyn:

You once said that if you flipped a coin 5 times, and it came up heads each time, the chances of it coming up heads the next time are 1 out of 2. Then just before the Super Bowl, the announcer flipped a coin, and it came up heads. He said that in practicing the flip before the game, they flipped the coin 5 times, and it came up heads all 5 times. He said the chances of this happening were only 1 out of 68. Who is right?

Sharon Broadway
Toledo, Ohio

Before you flip the coin at all, the chances of getting 6 heads in a row are 1 out of 64. But after you've flipped it 5 times (no matter what result you've received), the chances of the next flip producing a head are 1 out of 2. That is, it's easier to get 1 future heads toss than it is to get 6 of them.

Dear Marilyn:

Let's say that a fellow throws a die. Then I throw one. What are the chances that I will throw a higher number than he did? Isn't this an even bet? If he throws a 1, there are five numbers higher (2, 3, 4, 5, and 6), but if he throws a 6, there are five numbers lower (1, 2, 3, 4, and 5). If he throws a 2, there are four numbers higher (3, 4, 5, and 6) and one number lower (1), but if he throws a 5, there are four numbers lower (1, 2, 3, and 4) and one number higher (6). And if he throws a 3, there are three numbers higher (4, 5, and 6) and two numbers lower (1 and 2), but if he throws a 4, there are three numbers lower (1, 2, and 3) and two numbers higher (5 and 6). It looks the same to me, but my wife thinks I was taken.

Thomas Smith
Langhorne, Pennsylvania

You were taken, all right. The chances are only 5 out of 12 (not 6 out of 12, which is an even bet); you'll lose money if you play this game repeatedly. After the other fellow throws his die, there's 1 chance in 6 (which is the same as 2 chances in 12) that you'll then throw that *same number* (because there are six numbers on a die). This leaves only 5 chances out of 6 (or 10 chances out of 12) that you'll throw another number. Half of that time, you'll throw a higher number (5 times out of 12); the other half, you'll throw a lower number (5 times out of 12).

Dear Marilyn:

There is a puzzle every week in our local newspaper, and one's entry must be 100 percent correct to win. I recently found out that the newspaper has a unique way of determining the five winners. Rather than going through all the entries and sorting out the totally correct ones first, the people who run the competition just start drawing from the whole group, discarding those with an error, and they draw until they find five that are 100 percent correct. Are the odds different this way? It seems that if I had the puzzle correct, sorting the entries would increase my chances of winning.

Don Thorp
Springfield, Illinois

The chances are the same either way. Let's say there are 1,000 entries, of which 50 are totally correct and thus eligible to be winners. Whether they're sorted out neatly or covered with a truckload of confetti, there are still 50 of them. If your entry is correct, and 5 correct entries will win, you have 5 chances in 50 of being among those winners. The incorrect entries are as ineligible (and therefore irrelevant) as that confetti.

Dear Marilyn:

I've only tried gambling a few times (on vacation) in my life, but it occurs to me that the best way to win would be to observe a roulette wheel and wait until there's a long run of one color, then bet on the other color. (I did this once, and it worked.) For example, if red has come up twenty times, wouldn't it be much more likely for black to come up on the next spin?

Bob Billingsley
Oceanside, California

No. This is a classic example of what's known as the "gambler's fallacy," and some form of the error is found in numerous betting systems, even with experienced bettors. The key to understanding the mistake is realizing that the bettor has a memory, but the ivory ball does not. That is, there is a fifty-fifty chance that the ball will wind up in a black slot every time the wheel turns, regardless of where the ball wound up the last time, the time before, or the time before that. So if you place a bet whenever you observe red come up twenty times, you'll win half of the time and lose the other half of the time.

To convince yourself of the error in the "gambler's fallacy," envision this. You enter a gambling house, walk up to a roulette wheel, and place a bet that black will come up. Your chances of winning are fifty-fifty, right? Then the woman standing next to you announces that the last twenty spins came up black, so she's going to bet on red. How could the odds be different for the two of you?

Dear Marilyn:

Not long ago, you answered a question about a roulette wheel that has only black and red colors and stated, "There is a fifty-fifty chance that the ball will wind up in a black slot every time the wheel turns, regardless of where the ball wound up the last time, the time before, or the time before that." Do you know the chances if the wheel also has green spaces marked "0" and "00"?

Raymond Feinberg
New Braunfels, Texas

If there are 18 black slots, 18 red ones, and 2 green ones in an American roulette wheel, the chances that the ball will end up in a black slot are about 47.37 percent, the chances that it will end up in a red slot are about 47.37 percent, and it will wind up in a green slot about 5.26 percent of the time. Although you can still bet on the green slots directly, their presence tips the odds against the black/red bettors (and in favor of the gambling house). In Europe, however, where roulette originated, the wheels usually have only *one* green slot, which gives better odds to the bettors there (although still in favor of the casino overall).

Dear Marilyn:

Let's say that after a wonderful life here on Earth, you find yourself standing at the Pearly Gates in front of St. Peter. You are informed that to get inside, you must predict the outcome of the next spin of a black/red roulette wheel. You are also informed that the last 20 spins have ended in black. Although I know you're correct when you say that the odds are still fifty-fifty on each spin, I would side with probability here and choose red. Which would you choose?

Ray Henz, Sr.
Dillsburg, Pennsylvania

Probability does *not* point to red, even after 20 black spins. It says that the chances are equal on the next spin. But because that's the case, I'd choose black. Say St. Peter informs you that the last 20 *million* spins ended in black. Would you still choose red? Or would you suspect that the wheel is being controlled? (Maybe God is trying to make it easy for us, Ray!)

Look at it this way. Say you flip a coin and it comes up heads 200 times. Would you choose tails the next time? Or would you suspect that the coin is unevenly weighted? The same goes for only 20 flips. Because probability says that the chances are equal with a fair coin, you lose nothing by betting on heads just in case it *isn't* a fair coin. And each time heads comes up, the chances increase that the coin isn't fair.

Dear Marilyn:

I haven't missed a lotto drawing for years, twice a week and always using the same sets of numbers. If I continue as long as I can, what are my chances of winning, and how much better do my chances get with each miss?

Scott Engle
Aurora, Colorado

Your chances aren't improving at all. Any one set of numbers has the same chance of winning as any other set. This is because the lottery has no memory. That is, let's say I find a coin and decide to flip it. The chances are 50 percent that it'll land heads up, right? Now let's further suppose that when I found the coin, it was lying tails up after a previous coin flip. Does that make you change your mind and believe that the chances are now 100 percent that it'll land heads up? No. Like the lottery, the coin has no memory.

Dear Marilyn:

Since last February, I've been recording local winning lottery numbers. Is there some way I can analyze these numbers to come up with a potentially winning number?

Leona Robinson
Nashville, Arkansas

Not as far as probability is concerned. However, there have been cases in which the selection equipment has been faulty, with the result that certain numbers were winners more often than they would have been if all factors had been equal. For example, back in 1886, at a casino in Monte Carlo, a man named Joseph Hobson Jagger suspected that one of the roulette wheels had an imperfect spindle, so he quietly observed it for a few days. After verifying that certain numbers won too often, he began to bet on them and managed to win more than two million francs over the next week. Some people say that Jagger was the first "man who broke the bank at Monte Carlo," now immortalized in song.

Dear Marilyn:

I have a question about probability. I understand that the chances of any five numbers being chosen in a lottery would be the same, even if the numbers are 1,2,3,4,5. My question is, why does it *seem* to us so much more unlikely for 1,2,3,4,5 to be chosen than for five non-sequential numbers?

David Griggs-Janower
Schenectady, New York

Because you chose a *particular* sequence (1,2,3,4,5), but not any one particular non-sequential set (like 5,49,22,7,46). In other words, you compared *one* sequential set with *all* non-sequential sets.

All told, though, there are fewer sequential sets than there are non-sequential sets, so they're likely to win less often as a group. (If you put ten yellow fish and twenty blue fish in an aquarium, then scoop one out with a net, you're more likely to get a blue fish.) But the chances for any one sequential set are the same as for any one non-sequential set. (If you have one yellow fish named Tom, and two blue fish named

Dick and Harry, and you scoop one up, each has a one-third chance of feeling like a fish out of water.)

❌

Dear Marilyn:
Our state lottery has a weekly television show. After elimination rounds, one contestant is given the opportunity to win $1 million. The contestant picks from four hidden windows. Behind each window is one of the following: $150,000, $200,000, $1 million, or a "stopper." The contestant is allowed to keep picking a window until either $1 million is won or the "stopper" is picked, in which case nothing is won.

Before playing this final round, the contestant is offered $100,000 cash to stop there. The same applies to the windows; the contestant can either keep the cash contents of the chosen window and stop there, or he or she can pick a new window. Speaking only statistically, would a contestant be better off to take the $100,000 cash and not play the final round at all?

Douglas Offutt
Newburgh, Indiana

Statistically speaking, contestants should play the final round, at least to choosing one window; their chances of winning a significantly larger prize (than $100,000) are 3 out of 4 for the first choice. If every contestant chose one window and stopped there, the lottery would pay out an average of $337,500 per round. (Getting all the way through to the $1 million is much tougher, of course.)

But "statistically" is not the only way to speak. What's good for all contestants (as a group) is not necessarily what's good for each one individually. In other words, the same contestant will not be playing the final round again and again and thus will not be able to gain from average payouts over time. So if you're just *one* of those contestants, you would be wise to consider the risk versus the reward.

This will illustrate the risk-versus-reward situation of having chosen first the $150,000 window and then the $200,000 window: Say you own a $200,000 house with no mortgage. (That is, the $200,000 behind the window is yours to keep.) Would you put it at risk in a friendly dice game for a fifty-fifty chance of either turning it into a $1,000,000 house (by choosing the $1 million window) or losing it entirely (by choosing the "stopper")? I hope not; that would rank as an *extremely* risky investment.

And so is risking $100,000 for even a 3-out-of-4 chance at improvement. If I were you, I would take the $100,000 and choose the window at my neighborhood bank.

Dear Marilyn:

Last year I missed winning the Virginia lottery by only one number. (I chose five out of six numbers correctly.) Can you say something to make me feel better?

Mary Baumgardner
Lynchburg, Virginia

Mary, if I knew how to answer this question, we wouldn't need lotteries anymore.

Thirteen

On Math Problems

"This chapter will keep you
up half the night. . . ."

Dear Marilyn:

   Let's say that my friend and I run a 50-yard dash, and he crosses the finish 5 yards ahead of me. So we run the same race again, but this time he handicaps himself by starting 5 yards behind the starting line. If we run the second race at the same constant speed as we ran the first race, who will win?

Dan Brothe
Kent, Ohio

Your friend will win again. Judging from the first race, your friend runs 50 yards in the time you run 45. So if he starts 5 yards behind the starting line, you and he will draw even at the 45-yard point. But as the race is 50 yards long, and he runs faster than you do, he'll win again. By the time he runs the last 5 yards, you'll only have run 4.5, so he'll cross the 50-yard finish line when you're still at the 49.5-yard mark. If he wanted to even the race, he should have handicapped himself by allowing *you* to start 5 yards *ahead* of the starting line.

Dear Marilyn:

   My friend and I step onto an "up" escalator together. I walk up the moving escalator while he stands to the side and enjoys the ride. As soon as I reach the top, the escalator stops. I look back, and he is halfway down. He then walks up the remaining distance. If my friend and I walk up steps at the same rate, which of us walks up the most steps to reach the top of the escalator?

Alan Featherstone
Springfield, Virginia

You both walk up an equal number of steps. Let's say there are a hundred steps on the escalator, and it takes a minute for the bottom step to reach the top. Let's also say that's how fast the two of you climb steps— a hundred per minute. Adding your speed to the moving escalator's speed, you'll reach the top in half a minute; during that time, you'll have climbed fifty steps. Your friend, down at the halfway mark when the escalator stops, will therefore have to climb fifty more steps to reach you.

Dear Marilyn:

A barrel of water and a stone, placed side by side, together weigh 100 pounds. If you place the stone in the barrel (and the water does not overflow), will the total weight be less than 100 pounds, more, or the same? I encountered this question on a job aptitude test and have yet to find the answer anywhere.

David Maddox
Roanoke, Virginia

The total weight will stay 100 pounds. And if the stone is a live 5-pound trout instead, and he begins to swim, there will still be no change in weight. Even if you lower the fish into the water on a line until he's just barely submerged, the weight will remain the same. (For this purpose, we assumed that a given volume of fish weighs about the same as that volume of water.) But if you lower a 5-pound *stone* into the water on a line the same way, the total weight will *decrease* by about 2.5 pounds. (For this purpose, we assumed that a given volume of stone weighs about twice as much as that volume of water.) Odd, isn't it?

Dear Marilyn:

There are two candidates in an election and 100 voters, who all vote. The final result is 55 votes for Candidate A and 45 votes for Candidate B. By how many votes did Candidate B lose? If you say 10, consider this: Candidate B only needs to obtain 5 more votes for a tie and 6 votes to win. Therefore, didn't Candidate B only lose by 5 votes?

John Anderson
Portland, Oregon

I still think B lost by 10 because people aren't required by law to vote. As many as 9 of A's supporters could have stayed in bed that day, and B still would have lost—46 to 45. (Or would you call that losing by half a vote?!)

Dear Marilyn:

Could you please explain the following item, related by a man in a speech at a college on being presented with an award? He said that his father loves to tease his great-grandchildren by asking them this question: If one milk bottle is twice as big as another milk bottle, how much more milk will it hold? The speaker said that the kids would usually say "twice as much," and went on to ask the audience how many of them would agree. But then he said that "the right answer is eight times as much." How can that be the case?

Anonymous
Clarksburg, West Virginia

It can't—if a milk bottle is twice as big, that means the size in which it holds twice as much milk as the other one. However, it would have been a fair question if his father had asked, "Suppose a one-inch cube holds a certain amount of milk. How much milk would a two-inch cube hold?" It sounds similar, but the answer to *that* question is "eight times as much." You can demonstrate this with blocks. Say that one block represents the one-inch cube. To make a two-inch cube, then, you'll need two square layers of four blocks each, one layer on top of the other. (And it's eight times as big, not twice as big.)

Dear Marilyn:

If you slice a circle all the way across with one straight cut, you slice it into two pieces; with two straight cuts, you can slice it into four pieces. What is the maximum number of pieces you can get with ten cuts?

Rob Billings
La Jolla, California

You can get 56 pieces at the most. Here's a general rule.

1 cut can produce 2 pieces		6 cuts can produce 22 pieces
2 cuts can produce 4 pieces		7 cuts can produce 29 pieces
3 cuts can produce 7 pieces		8 cuts can produce 37 pieces
4 cuts can produce 11 pieces		9 cuts can produce 46 pieces
5 cuts can produce 16 pieces		10 cuts can produce 56 pieces

Note that each additional cut produces that same number of more pieces to add to the maximum number of pieces produced by the previous cut. (For example, 4 cuts can produce 11 pieces, so for 5 cuts, just add 5 to 11: 5 cuts can produce 16 pieces. And so on with more cuts.) The reason is that each additional cut can always be placed in such a way so as to cross all the previous cuts. Parents who want to drive their kids crazy might suggest that they try it.

Dear Marilyn:

You go to a carnival where there are two booths tended by honest men. Each booth contains a pair of covered coin shakers. In each shaker is a single coin, and you are allowed to bet upon the chance that both coins in that booth's shakers are heads after the man in the booth shakes them, does an inspection, and can tell you that at least one of the shakers contains a head. The difference is that the man in the first booth always looks inside both his shakers, whereas the man in the second booth looks inside only one of his shakers. Where will you stand the best chance?

Daniel Hahn
Blairstown, Iowa

You have the best chance in the second booth, where the man looks at only one of his shakers. The chances that both coins are heads in the first booth are one in three; the chances that both are heads in the second booth are one in two.

Dear Marilyn:

A friend recently bet me $100 to my dime that if I cut a deck of cards into five piles, there would be an even number of piles that contain odd numbers of cards in each pile, and an odd number of piles that contain even numbers of cards in each pile. I stopped playing after I lost a dollar. Why did he always win?

George Groth
Hendersonville, North Carolina

Because 1 or 3 or 5 odd piles would always add up to an odd number of cards, and 2 or 4 even piles would always add up to an even number of cards. An odd number plus an even number equals an odd number of cards, but there is an *even* number of cards in a deck (52 in a regular deck, 54 with jokers, and 48 in a pinochle deck). So no matter how you divide the cards into 5 piles, there must be either no odd piles at all or 2 odd piles or 4 of them. And as that's the case, that leaves only 1, 3, and 5 for the number of even piles. (When there are no odd piles, there are 5 even ones. When there are 2 odd piles, there are 3 even ones. And when there are 4 odd piles, there is 1 even one.)

Dear Marilyn:

I have a really confusing one for you. Let's say my friend puts six playing cards facedown on a table. He tells me that exactly two of them are aces. Then I get to pick up two of the cards. Which of the following two choices is the most likely?

 (A) That I'll get one or both of the aces.
 (B) That I'll get no aces.

Darryl Button
New Orleans, Louisiana

The answer is (A)—it's more likely that you'll get one or both of the aces. Let's say the cards are numbered 1 through 6, with 3 and 4 as the aces. Here are the fifteen possible combinations you might get:

1 & 2	1 & 3	1 & 4	1 & 5	1 & 6
	2 & 3	2 & 4	2 & 5	2 & 6
		3 & 4	3 & 5	3 & 6
			4 & 5	4 & 6
				5 & 6

Picking any one of those combinations is as likely as picking any other. Note that 3 or 4 (the aces) appear in nine of the combinations, which is more than half of them. Therefore, it's more likely that you'll get one or both of the aces than no aces at all.

Dear Marilyn:

The following problem baffles me. Take an ordinary deck of 52 cards and shuffle it. Then turn the cards over one at a time, counting as you go, ace, two, three, and so on, until you reach king, then start over again. The object is to turn over all 52 cards without having your spoken number match the card you turn over at the time. Easy, right? Well, it sounded easy to me, too. I figured that for each card you turn over, you have only a 1-in-13 chance of it matching your count (because there are 13 different card values.) But it does not seem to work that way. In hundreds of tries, I have only succeeded once! Please explain this to me. Am I looking at the odds wrong? (Please don't go crazy trying this; ask someone else to do it!)

Charles Price
Lakeland, Florida

Your odds are right, but you're stretching them too thin. In addition to going through 12 out of 13 *cards* without a match, you're hoping to go through 12 out of 13 *decks* without a match. That is, when you have a 1-in-13 chance of each card matching your count, this means that the event will happen about once in every 13 turns of a card. But you're expecting to turn over 52 cards without it happening, which will seldom be the case. Instead, you'll average 4 matches in every deck.

Dear Marilyn:
    You have six envelopes to choose from. Two-thirds of them (that is, 4) are empty. One-third of them (that is, 2) contain a $100 bill. You're allowed to choose two envelopes at random. Which is more likely: (1) that you'll get at least one $100 bill, or (2) that you'll get no $100 bill at all?

Bill Bollinger
Sun City West, Arizona

It's more likely that you'll get at least one $100 bill. Let's label the envelopes from No. 1 through No. 6 and say that No. 2 and No. 4 contain the $100 bills. Here are the 15 possible pairs of envelopes you could choose:

1 & 2	2 & 3	3 & 4	4 & 5	5 & 6
1 & 3	2 & 4	3 & 5	4 & 6	
1 & 4	2 & 5	3 & 6		
1 & 5	2 & 6			
1 & 6				

    Notice that No. 2 or No. 4 appear in 9 of the 15 pairs, which is more than a fifty-fifty chance. In fact, your chance of getting at least one $100 bill is quite high: 60 percent.

Dear Marilyn:

   A nanny with four small children passes a bubble-gum machine, and all four beg for a gumball. However, the nanny knows they will cry unless they all receive the same color. The machine is almost empty, and she can count 8 pink gumballs, 6 blue ones, and 1 green one. At a penny per ball, how much money is the most she might have to spend in order to get four matching gumballs?

                                        Lou Chough
                                        Bentonville, Arkansas

8 cents. With the worst possible luck, the nanny could spend 7 cents and end up with 3 pink gumballs, 3 blue ones, and the 1 green one. With a penny more, then, the next gumball would be either pink or blue, making the fourth match.

Dear Marilyn:

   I am writing to find out if I have a marital problem. My wife does the laundry in our house weekly. I have two pairs of argyle socks, and they look nearly identical—one navy blue and the other black. My wife matches the socks incorrectly much more often than she does correctly. Is this due to subconscious resentment? If all four socks are in front of her, and she picks up two at the same time, it seems to me that her chances are 50 percent for a wrong match and 50 percent for a right match. What do you think?

                                        Brad Evans
                                        Birmingham, Alabama

On chance alone, the socks will match incorrectly two-thirds of the time. Let's label them Navy #1, Navy #2, Black #1, and Black #2. The possible pairings are as follows:

1) Navy #1 + Navy #2   Black #1 + Black #2   (match)
2) Navy #1 + Black #1   Navy #2 + Black #2   (no match)
3) Navy #1 + Black #2   Navy #2 + Black #1   (no match)

   And it's your wife who has the marital problem if you only have two pairs of socks!

Dear Marilyn:

Can you help me out with the following problem? Let's say that half the employees in a firm went to lunch at noon. Since then, 25 have returned, and 7 others have gone out. At this point, there are twice as many people working as there are people out to lunch. How many people are employed at the firm in all?

Bill Saltzman
St. Louis, Missouri

There are 108 mouths to feed. Half of them (54) went to lunch at noon. Then 25 returned, and 7 left. At this point, there are twice as many people working (the 54 who remained, plus the 25 who returned, minus the 7 who left, a total of 72) as there are people lunching (the 54 who went to lunch, minus the 25 who returned, plus the 7 who left later, a total of 36).

Dear Marilyn:

Let's say a company sells candy bars with basketball team names imprinted on the bar, and there are 27 teams. If I can't open the wrappers beforehand, how many candy bars would I have to buy to make sure I have a full set?

Michael Rose
Salona, Pennsylvania

It depends on the number of candy bars produced and the number of times each team is imprinted on one. That is, if there are 27,000 candy bars, but only one of them bears team No. 1, you might wind up opening 26,999 wrappers only to look up and see your best friend taking a big bite out of the Chicago Bulls. But let's assume the candy company has imprinted 1,000 candy bars for each team. You still might find yourself with 26,000 bars that almost make 1,000 sets, but don't quite make even one. You'd have to buy 26,001 to be sure.

Dear Marilyn:

This problem appeared in our local newspaper. "If each of 10 little-league baseball teams played each of the other teams twice, how many games would there be?" The National Council of Teachers of Mathematics says the answer is 90. Shouldn't the correct answer be 180 games?

John Lowden
Wilmington, North Carolina

Ninety is correct. Let's reduce the number of teams to 4 (a total of 12 games, not 24) in order to see the reason more clearly.

A plays B	A plays D	B plays D
A plays B	A plays D	B plays D
A plays C	B plays C	C plays D
A plays C	B plays C	C plays D

The reason the number is only half what we'd expect is that when A plays B (etc.), B plays A at the same time (that is, during the same game). So one game suffices for both teams.

Dear Marilyn:

It took me 45 minutes to solve this, but I'll bet you can do it in 5. Three schools have a track meet and enter one person in each event. The number of events is unknown, and so is the scoring system except that the winner of each event scores a certain number of points, second place scores fewer points, and third places scores fewer still. Georgia won with 22, and Alabama and Florida tied with 9 each. Florida won the High Jump. Who won the Mile Run?

Kenton Creuser
Atlanta, Georgia

Georgia did.

Because 40 points are tallied at the meet, there are no more than 6 events. (The lowest possible scoring system of 3, 2, and 1 produces 42 points with 7 events.) So the number of events must range from 2 through 6.

Given that, there must be 2, 4, or 5 events. (The 40 points tallied cannot be divided evenly by 3 or 6 events.) So 2 events produce 20 points each, or 4 events produce 10 points each, or 5 events produce 8 points each.

Because Florida scored 9 for the meet, the highest score possible for a single event is 8 points. (There are at least 2 events, and Florida won at least 1, but it would have scored at least 1 point for the other event, even if it finished third.) So the number of points ranges from 3 through 8 for first place, from 2 through 7 for second, and from 1 through 6 for third.

Given that, there must be 4 or 5 events. (If there had been only 2 events and Florida won 1 of them, the most Georgia could have scored was 15—for a first and second place—not 22.)

With at least 4 events in the meet, a first place must be worth no more than 6 points. (Florida won at least 1, but it would have scored at least 1 point for the others, even if it finished third.) So the scoring must range from 3 to 6 for first place, from 2 to 5 for second, and from 1 to 4 for third.

Given that range, these are the possible scoring systems.

4 events at 10 points each:

A) 6 for first place, 3 for second place, 1 for third place
B) 5 for first place, 4 for second place, 1 for third place
C) 5 for first place, 3 for second place, 2 for third place

5 events at 8 points each:

D) 5 for first place, 2 for second place, 1 for third place

But because Florida tallied 9 points for the whole meet, B and C are impossible. (With 4 events, including a win, Florida's score would either top 9 or not add up to it.) And because Georgia tallied 22 points for the whole meet, A is impossible. (With 4 events, Georgia's score would top 22 with 4 first places, and its score wouldn't reach 22 with any other combination.)

So there must be 5 events at 8 points each, 5 for first place, 2 for second place, and 1 for third place. Given that, Florida must have scored 1 first place (the High Jump) and 4 third places. (With any second places, Florida's score would have topped 9.) And Georgia must have scored 4 first places and 1 second place. (With only 3 first places, Georgia's score wouldn't have reached 22.) And so Alabama must have scored 4 second places and 1 third place. Which means that Georgia must have won the Mile Run.

You lose the bet. It took me about 22 minutes, much longer than you thought. How much do I win?

Dear Marilyn:

A man in a canoe paddles upstream from a dock for one mile and throws a float out. He rows farther upstream for ten minutes, then turns around and rows back downstream to the dock. He arrives there at exactly the same time that the float does. What is the speed of the current?

David Arey
Hobe Sound, Florida

Three miles per hour. Because the float was thrown into the water a mile upstream, it traveled that mile (back down to the dock) in a certain period of time. What was that period? Well, the man rowed upstream for ten minutes after throwing it, then rowed downstream (back down to the dock) in another ten minutes. How do we know about that second ten minutes? Assuming that he rowed at the same speed (which means that rowing upstream would slow him relative to the shoreline, and rowing downstream would speed him the same way), however far away from the float he could row in ten minutes, he could return to the float in the same amount of time. This is why:

Envision a revolving carousel with wooden horses. You stand next to a red horse and walk away from it "upstream" for five seconds at your normal pace. Say you're now standing next to the blue horse in back of the red one. How long would it take you to walk back "downtsream" to the red horse? Another five seconds. That's because you and the horses are together on the same moving carousel. That's the way it is with the float and the canoe. They're both on the same moving river.

So the float traveled that one mile back down to the dock in twenty minutes (while the man rowed upstream for ten minutes and downstream for ten more). And traveling one mile in twenty minutes is the same as three miles per hour.

Dear Marilyn:

Two alien spacecraft are traveling directly toward each other, one at 38,171 miles per hour and the other at 21,829 miles per hour. They originated on planets 82,710,317 miles apart. Without using paper and pencil to get the answer, how far apart will they be a minute before they collide?

Mike Androtti
Ely, Minnesota

A thousand miles. The distance between their home planets is irrelevant. The two spacecraft are approaching each other at a combined speed of 60,000 miles per hour (38,171 mph + 21,829 mph = 60,000 mph), which means the distance between them is closing at 1,000 miles per minute (60,000 mph ÷ 60 minutes in an hour = 1,000 miles per minute). So a minute before the collision, they'd have to be 1,000 miles apart.

Dear Marilyn:

Let's say there are two suitcases filled with money on the table. One bag contains 50 pounds of $100 bills. The other bag contains 100 pounds of $50 bills. Which one would you choose?

R. E. Moore
Edgewater, Florida

I'd choose the suitcase that goes best with the rest of my luggage at home because the value of their contents is the same. If there's no difference in the weight of the ink, the 100-pound bag must contain twice as many bills as the 50-pound bag, which means that there must be two $50 bills for every one $100 bill.

Dear Marilyn:

When are you going to answer my question?! What's your excuse? You once wrote that you get enough questions each week to fill an entire magazine, and that you don't get enough space to answer them all. If that's the case, then stop asking for more questions! Mine must be at the bottom of the pile. I'd hate to see how big that pile of questions really is. You must have trunks full. Where do you keep them all? My question is about a ship and its boiler. A ship is twice as old as its boiler was when the ship was as old as the boiler is. The sum of their ages is 49. How old is the ship, and how old is the boiler? Please answer soon.

This is the third letter I've written after I sent you the question the first time.

Domnick Cerra

Dunmore, Pennsylvania

You may regret this, Domnick. Say that S is the age of the ship now; B is the age of the boiler now. Because S+B=49, then S=49-B. So because S is "twice as old as its boiler was when the ship was as old as the boiler is," then 49-B is "twice as old as its boiler was when the ship was as old as" B. Continuing this substitution, 49-B is two times an earlier boiler age. How do we define this earlier age?

The age difference in years between the ship and the boiler always remains the same. So back at this earlier age, the boiler's age would have been the ship's earlier age of B ("when the ship was as old as the boiler is [now]" minus the number of years that the ship and the boiler are always apart. That "apart" number of years could be expressed as the ship's age minus the boiler's age, even now. So because the ship is now 49-B years old (now), and the boiler is B years old (now), that age difference can be expressed as (49-B)-(B). Therefore, the boiler's earlier age can be expressed as B minus (49-B)-(B).

Rewritten, 49-B is 2 times as old as (B-[(49-B)-(B)]).
Which means the same as 49-B=2(B-[(49-B)-(B)]).
Solving, we see that 49-B=2(B-[49-2B]).
Which is the same as 49-B=2(B-49+2B).
$$49-B=2 (3B-49)$$
$$49-B=6B-98$$
$$147=7B$$
$$21=B$$

And if the boiler (B) is 21 years old, the ship (S) is 28. (But at least my bathtub is lighter by 4 letters.)

Dear Marilyn:

I think this is a "trick question," but here it is. A certain battalion had between two and three thousand men. They wanted to divide the battalion into not more than nine groups, each containing the same number of men. However, it was discovered that it couldn't be done because there was always one man left over. How many men were in the battalion?

Ruth Zuberer
Wayne, New Jersey

Let's represent the missing number by 2XXX, standing for the possible range from 2001 through 2999. First, the only numbers divisible by 5 (remembering that the number of men in the battalion couldn't be evenly divided into 5 groups) end in 0 or 5. For this reason (also remembering that a division of men into 5 groups would have 1 left over), the number of men in the battalion must end in 1 or 6. But any number ending in 6 can be divided by 2 (and the men couldn't be divided into 2 groups, either), so the number must end in 1, instead. (That is, 2XX1.)

However, in addition to being divisible by 5 with one left over, the number must be divisible by 9 with one left over. So let's subtract 1 from 2XX1 and work with the number 2XX0, instead. All the numbers from 2010 through 2990 that end in 0 *and* are evenly divisible by 9 are possibilities for being just one short of the number of men in the battalion.

Knowing that for a number to be divisible by 9, the sum of its digits must be divisible by 9, this eliminates most of the remaining numbers. Here are the only ones left:

2070	2610
2160	2700
2250	2790
2340	2880
2430	2970
2520	

Remember, we're still looking for the number that must be evenly divisible by each number from 2 through 9. (The actual number of men will be 1 more.) We've already dealt with divisors of 2, 5, and 9. Any number divisible by 9 is also divisible by 3, so we've dealt with 3; and any even number divisible by 3 is also divisible by 6, so we've dealt with 6, too. This leaves 4, 7, and 8 still to be considered.

Knowing that for a number to be divisible by 4, the last two digits must be 00 or be divisible by 4, this eliminates more numbers. Here are the only ones left:

2160   2340   2520   2700   2880

It's a simple matter to divide these remaining numbers by 7, leaving only 2520 as a possibility. And because 2520 is divisible by our last remaining unchecked divisor of 8, it must indeed be the "divisible" number. (That is, 2520 is evenly divisible by 2, 3, 4, 5, 6, 7, 8, and 9.) So there must be 2521 men in the battalion. Wherever you divide them—from two through nine groups—there's always one left over.

It doesn't sound like a trick question to me, but maybe I'm missing something. I suppose you could say that the number of men ranged from two (instead of two *thousand*) to three thousand, but there are no numbers under 2000 that satisfy the conditions.

Dear Marilyn:

Joe Smith received a license plate for his new car. He noted that all five digits were different, and that if the plate were upside down, his registration number would be increased by 7920. What was the number on the license plate?

Bill Henning
Dubuque, Iowa

Using the digits 0 through 9, the license number could be either 60189 (increasing to 68109 upside down) or 90186 (increasing to 98106 upside down), and here's how to get it.

2, 3, 4, 5, and 7 don't work upside down (they neither stay the same nor turn into other numbers), so the license number must be made of 0, 1, 6, 8, and 9 (because five different digits are required). Assuming that no number can start with 0, the license number can't end with 0, either. And it doesn't start with 1 because any upside-down view (with 6, 8, or 9 on the end) would show more than a 7920 difference. It also can't end with 1 because any upside-down view would get smaller, not larger. Furthermore, it doesn't start with 8 because the end number would have to be 6 (the only number that gets larger when upside down), and none of those six combinations (80196, 80916, 81096,

81906, 89016, or 89106) increase by 7920 when viewed upside down. It also can't end with 8 because the beginning number would have to be 6 (9XXX8 would be more than 8XXX6, not less), and the difference between 6XXX8 and 8XXX9 is more than 7920.

That leaves 6 and 9 for starting and ending numbers. The second number in each case can't be 8 because the whole number would decrease (instead of increase) upside down. This leaves only four combinations for each (60189, 60819, 61089, or 61809, and 90186, 90816, 91086, or 91806), so without further thinking, you can just turn them upside down to discover that two of them do indeed increase by the requisite 7920.

Dear Marilyn:
    Can you figure this one out?
                    USSR + USA = PEACE
    (Each letter stands for a different number.)

                                        Rachael Harris
                                        Mount Vernon, Indiana

P must be 1 because even if USSR were as high as 9887 and USA were as high as 986, PEACE couldn't be higher than 10873. For the same reason, E must be 0. And U must be 9 because even if USSR were as high as 8997 and USA were as high as 896, PEACE wouldn't be a five-digit number. So 9SSR + 9SA = 10AC0.

S cannot be 8 because even if USSR were as low as 9882 and USA were as low as 983, PEACE would have to be at least 10865, but A can't be 8 at the same time. S cannot be 7 because even if USSR were as low as 9772 and USA were as low as 973, PEACE would have to be at least 10745, but A can't be 7 at the same time. S cannot be 6 because even if USSR were as low as 9662 and USA were as low as 963, PEACE would have to be at least 10625, but A can't be 6 at the same time. S cannot be 5 because even if USSR were as low as 9552 and USA were as low as 953, PEACE would have to be at least 10505, but A can't be 5 at the same time. On the other hand, S cannot be 2 because even if USSR were as high as 9228 and USA were as high as 927, PEACE couldn't be higher than 10155, but A can't be 1.

So S is either 3 or 4. If S is 3, A is 2 because 9332 to 9338 + 932 to 938 = 10264 to 10276. If S is 4, A is 3 because 9442 to 9448 + 942 to

948 = 10384 to 10396. This means either that S is 3 and A is 2 or that S is 4 and A is 3.

But if S is 4 and A is 3, R would be 7 and C would be 9, which is impossible because U is already 9. So S is 3 and A is 2, which means that R is 8 and C is 7. The only possible answer, then, is 9338 + 932 = 10270.

Fourteen

On Logic Puzzles

"... And this chapter will keep
you up for the <u>other</u> half!"

Dear Marilyn:

A king, wishing to get rid of his prime minister, put two pieces of paper in a hat. He tells a judge present that if the prime minister draws out the scrap marked "stay," he may remain in the kingdom, but if he draws the scrap marked "go," he must scram. The hitch is, the king wrote "go" on both scraps of paper. But when the crafty prime minister showed the judge one of the pieces of paper, the judge decided in his favor. How did the prime minister outwit the king?

Silas Culver
Evansville, Indiana

The prime minister removed a slip of paper, saw that it read "go," and then, hoping that the king had limited powers of logic, gulped it down before anyone could get to him. (At this point, at least it was worth a try.) The judge sighed and said, "What a silly prime minister! I'll just look at the *other* slip of paper." It read "go," so the judge assumed the prime minister's paper had read "stay." And because the king didn't want to embarrass himself by admitting what he'd done, the prime minister remained happily in power until the monarchy was brought down by one personal scandal after another, at which point a general election was held, and the citizens dumped the prime minister themselves.

Dear Marilyn:

A room contains three exposed light bulbs. Three switches, each controlling one bulb, are outside the room. The room's door is closed. You are outside and cannot see into the room. Your problem is to determine which switch controls which bulb. You are allowed to go into the room, but once you have opened the door, you may not touch the switches.

Mitch Bradley
Mountain View, California

You turn on switches No. 1 and No. 2 and turn off No. 3. Wait a few minutes, turn off No. 2 too, then go into the room and touch the two unlit bulbs. The warm one is controlled by switch No. 2, the other one is controlled by No. 3, and the lit one is controlled by No. 1.

Dear Marilyn:

I have a puzzle for you, but I'm not sure if I'm right about the answer. A man has a raft and three cantaloupes. Each cantaloupe weighs a pound. However, the raft can hold only 202 pounds, and the man weighs 200 pounds himself. How does the man get to the other side of the river with the cantaloupes? (His weight includes his clothes, nothing can get wet, and the cantaloupes can't be thrown across the river, etc.)

Micah Tussey
Yuma, Arizona

Nope, the cantaloupes can't be juggled (always keeping one in the air), and still keep the raft afloat. The force required to throw a cantaloupe upward over and over, combined with the downward force absorbed when it's caught again and again, will together increase the weight of the raft by an average of a pound. If the poor fellow, trying to juggle such things, envisions adding that to the other two cantaloupes, he'll definitely get a "sinking" feeling.

Dear Marilyn:

Four men and four women are shipwrecked on a desert island. Eventually, each one falls in love with one other, and is himself or herself loved by one person. John loves the woman who loves Jim. Arthur loves the woman who loves the man who loves Ellen. Mary is loved by the man who is loved by the woman who is loved by Bruce. Gloria hates Bruce and is hated by the man whom Hazel loves. Who loves Arthur?

The Fifth Grade Students
of Clyattville Elementary School
Valdosta, Georgia

I was tempted to say, "Arthur's mother," and leave my desk for the afternoon. This problem is conceptually disorganized. For example, it appears that we should assume that "Mary is loved by the man who is loved by the woman who is loved by Bruce" is not a convoluted way of saying that Mary and Bruce love each other. If so, then "Gloria hates Bruce and is hated by the man whom Hazel loves" should not mean simply that Gloria and Bruce hate each other. But that's indeed the case. By my reasoning, Gloria loves Arthur, who loves Hazel, who loves Bruce, who loves Ellen, who loves John, who loves Mary, who loves Jim, who loves Gloria. (It sounds very complicated now, I know, but this will begin to seem like a real-life situation by the time you get to the eighth grade.)

Dear Marilyn:

Four women, one of whom was known to have committed a terrible crime, made the following statements when questioned by the police.

Fawn: Kitty did it.
Kitty: Robin did it.
Bunny: I didn't do it.
Robin: Kitty lied.

If only one of these four statements is true, who was the guilty woman?

Barney Bissinger
Hershey, Pennsylvania

Bunny was guilty, and here's why.

Let's say Fawn told the truth. If so, Kitty did it. But then Bunny's and Robin's statements would be true, so that can't be the solution. So let's say Kitty told the truth instead. If so, Robin did it. But then Bunny's statement would be true, so that can't be the solution, either. So let's say Bunny told the truth instead. If so, Bunny didn't do it. And Kitty didn't do it (the lie from Fawn), Robin didn't do it (the lie from Kitty), and Bunny didn't do it (the truth from Bunny), leaving only Fawn as the culprit. But then Robin's statement would be true, so that can't be the solution, either.

So let's say Robin told the truth instead. If so, Kitty lied, and Robin didn't do it, Fawn lied, and Kitty didn't do it, and Bunny lied, meaning Bunny *did* do it. This is the only solution that works. If Bunny did it, Fawn lied when she said Kitty did it, Kitty lied when she said Robin did it, Bunny lied when she said she didn't do it, and Robin told the truth when she said Kitty lied.

And now I have a question for *you*. Suppose only one of the four statements is *false*. Who was the guilty woman then? (The answer is at the end of the chapter.)

Dear Marilyn:

Would you please solve this problem for me? Gardner, Plunkett, Maloney, Phelps, and Lopez work for the Littleville Fire Department. They each get two weeks' vacation per year. As it happens, last year they each took their first week in the first five months of the year and their second week in the last five months of the year. Remembering that each man took each of his weeks in a different month, try to determine the months in which each man took his first and second weeks. I'm stumped!

(1) Mr. Plunkett took his first week before Mr. Gardner, who took his before Mr. Phelps; for their second week, the order was reversed. (2) The man who vacationed in March also vacationed in September. (3) Mr. Lopez did not take his first week in April or in March. (4) Neither Mr. Lopez nor the man who took his first week in January took his second week in August or December. (5) Mr. Maloney took his second week before Mr. Plunkett but after Mr. Lopez.

Mrs. James Bunting
Red Bluff, California

No one vacationed in June or July. According to (3) and (4), Lopez did not vacation in January, March, April, August, or December. Because of (2), Lopez could not have vacationed in September, either; this leaves only October and November for his second week. According to (5), Maloney took his second week after Lopez, so Maloney must have vacationed in November or December. But also according to (5), Maloney took his second week before Plunkett, so Maloney must have vacationed in November, and Plunkett must have vacationed in December; this means that Lopez must have vacationed in October. And because of (1), Phelps must have vacationed in August, and Gardner must have vacationed in September. Perhaps the key to untangling this puzzle is noting that just because Plunkett took his first week before Gardner, who took his before Phelps (and the reverse for their second week) doesn't mean that they necessarily took them in *consecutive* order.

Because of (2), Gardner must have vacationed in March. And according to (4), neither Phelps nor Plunkett vacationed in January; this leaves only Maloney for that month. So (1) places Plunkett in February. And because Lopez didn't vacation in April, he must have vacationed in May; this leaves only Phelps for April, and sure enough, according to (1), he fits there nicely. So the vacations looked like this:

JAN	MALONEY	FEB	PLUNKETT
MAR	GARDNER	APR	PHELPS
MAY	LOPEZ	AUG	PHELPS
SEP	GARDNER	OCT	LOPEZ
NOV	MALONEY	DEC	PLUNKETT

Dear Marilyn:

Say that each Thanksgiving, my wife's cousins get together for dinner. There are five cousins in all, and each brings his or her spouse. One peculiarity is that every cousin always uses the middle name when referring to another cousin. When referring to non-cousins, the first name is used. The non-cousins always refer to everyone by their first name. Guests are seated at a table with five people on each side. My chair is in the middle of one side. Each person makes one statement to me, beginning with the person on my left and proceeding clockwise. The following statements are made:

No. 1: "My spouse is sitting between Lynn and Don."

No. 2: "I am Alice, and I married one of the cousins, Joe."

No. 3: "You are sitting next to Preston, my husband."

No. 4: "My wife Wilma is sitting directly across from Cheryl."

No. 5: "Of the cousins, Lynn is the tallest, I am next, then comes Carolyn, with Ann being the shortest."

No. 6: "I am Thomas, and my wife is Sarah."

No. 7: "My husband is Jack."

No. 8: "Beth is directly across from Raymond."

No. 9: "Mary is taller than Wilma but shorter than Raymond."

The seating is arranged such that each husband sits on the opposite side of the table from his wife, but no husband sits directly across from his wife. Also, no cousin sits next to another cousin. What are the cousins' names, and to whom is each married? What is my name?

Mr. Murphy
Cedar Rapids, Iowa

As you've enclosed a solution, I'm suspicious. Surely you don't expect me to publish your solution as my own, do you?! And then find out it's cleverly incorrect?! (I can't rest easy as long as there are postgraduate college students with extra time on their hands, you know.) So here it is, in my own words:

You're person No. 10. Because you're not a cousin, No. 1 or No. 2 (but not both, because they're seated together) may be a cousin, and No. 8 or No. 9 (again, but not both) may be a cousin. So there must be at least 3 cousins across the table. But because no cousin can sit next to another, their upper limit is 3, and they must be No. 3, No. 5, and No. 7. Person No. 2 states that she's married to a cousin, so person No. 1 must be a cousin. Person No. 3 states that you're sitting next to her husband, so No. 9 must not be a cousin. Which means No. 8 is a cousin. So now we know who's a cousin and who's not: Person No. 1 is a cousin, No. 2 is not, No. 3 is a cousin, No. 4 is not, No. 5 is a cousin, No. 6 is not, No. 7 is a cousin, No. 8 is a cousin (they're seated across from each other, not together), No. 9 is not, and neither are you (No. 10). And from the statements of No. 2, No. 3, and No. 6, we know that No. 2's name is Alice, No. 9's name is Preston, and No. 6's name is Thomas. And from the statements of No. 2, No. 3, No. 4, No. 6, and No. 7, we know that No. 2 is female, No. 3 is female, and No. 9 is male, No. 4 is male, No. 6 is male, and No. 7 is female, and we already know that No. 10 (you) is male. Okay so far?

From her statement, we know that No. 1 (a cousin) must be female because the only two non-cousins on the other side of the table are males. From the statement of No. 2 (a female non-cousin), we know that the first name of No. 5 must be Joe because the only other cousins on the other side of the table are also females. From the statement of No. 4 (a male non-cousin), we know that the first name of No. 8 must be Wilma because he's sitting directly across from the only other cousin; we also know that the first name of No. 7 must be Cheryl, who sits directly across from No. 8. From the statement of No. 6 (a male non-cousin), we know that the first name of No. 1 must be Sarah because she's the only female cousin on the other side left unnamed. From the statement of No. 7 (a female cousin), we know that your name (No. 10) is Jack because you're the only male non-cousin on the other side left unnamed. From the statement of No. 8, we know that the middle name of No. 1 is Beth because of the remaining individuals with missing names, No. 7 is directly across from a female, No. 5 is a male, and No. 3 is directly across from a female; we also know that the name of No. 4 must be Raymond, who sits directly across from No. 1. From the statement of No. 9 (a non-cousin), we know that the first name of No. 3 is Mary because she is the only individual with an unknown first name. You know, No. 10, this is a little longer than I'd expected.

We're now missing only the middle names of cousins No. 3, No. 5, No. 7, and No. 8. From the statement of No. 1 (a female cousin who can't be sitting across from her husband), we know that the middle name of No. 5 must be Don and that the middle name of No. 7 must be Lynn. And from the statement of No. 5 (a male cousin), we know that the middle names of No. 3 and No. 8 must be Carolyn and Ann (because no other cousin's names are missing), but we don't know which is which. We get that information by adding the statement of No. 9. So if Carolyn is taller than Ann (according to cousin No. 5), and Mary is taller than Wilma (according to non-cousin No. 9), the middle name of No. 3 must be Carolyn, and the middle name of No. 8 must be Ann. Goodness. We're not finished *yet*.

From No. 1, we learn that Sarah Beth is married to Thomas. From No. 2, Joe Don is married to Alice. From No. 3, Mary Carolyn is married to Preston. From No. 4, Wilma Ann is married to Raymond. And from No. 7, Cheryl Lynn is married to Jack. Now I'm going to peek at your answer, and if it's different from mine, I'm going to pack up my pencils and go home early.

Dear Marilyn:

Five different-color houses are in a row. Each is owned by a man of different nationality, hobby, pet, and favorite drink. The Englishman lives in the red house, the Spaniard owns dogs, coffee is drunk in the green house, the Ukrainian drinks tea, the green house is directly to the right of the white one, the stamp collector owns snails, the antique collector lives in the yellow house, the man in the middle house drinks milk, the Norwegian lives in the first house, the man who sings lives next to the man with the fox, the man who gardens drinks juice, the antique collector lives next to the man with the horse, the Japanese man's hobby is cooking, and the Norwegian lives next to the blue house. What I would like to know is, who drinks water, who owns the zebra, and how in the world did you figure this out??

Vinita Takiar
Baltimore, Maryland

Well, you definitely need a pencil for this one, Vinita. Here's one of the ways to figure it out. (Draw five houses and follow it along.) Coffee is drunk in the green house, so the Englishman doesn't drink it. The man who collects stamps owns snails, so he's not the Spaniard. The antique collector lives in the yellow house, so the Englishman has another hobby. The man who gardens drinks juice, so he's not the Ukrainian. The Norwegian, who lives in house No. 1, lives next to the blue house, which must be No. 2. The man who drinks juice gardens, so he's not the Japanese. The man who lives in the green house drinks coffee, so the Ukrainian doesn't live there. The man who owns snails collects stamps, so he's not the Japanese. (Hmmm. Maybe you'll need an eraser, too.)

The first house is owned by the Norwegian, so it's not red (whose owner is English), and it's not blue (which is next door), and it's not green or white (which are next to each other), so it's yellow. Coffee is drunk in the green house, and milk is drunk in the middle house, so the Norwegian doesn't drink either. The antique collector lives in the yellow house, so he's the Norwegian. He also lives next to the man with the horse, so the Spaniard doesn't live in the blue house. The man who drinks juice gardens, so he's not the Norwegian. *This means the Norwegian drinks water.*

The owner of the horse lives next to the antique collector, so the Norwegian doesn't own one; the owner of the horse also lives in the blue house, so the Englishman doesn't own one. The man who owns snails collects stamps, so the Norwegian doesn't own them. The green house is just to the right of the white one, so Nos. 3, 4, and 5 are red, white, and green, or else they're white, green, and red. If No. 5 is red, the Englishman lives there, and coffee is drunk in No. 4.

But the man who likes to garden drinks juice, and he can't live in No. 2 because the only two who can drink juice are the Englishman and the Spaniard, and neither can own a horse. Which would mean the Englishman gardens and drinks juice. Which would mean the Spaniard sings, and the Ukrainian collects stamps and own snails. Which would mean the Japanese owns the horse and lives in No. 2. Which would mean the Ukrainian lives in No. 3. But that can't be, can it?! The Ukrainian drinks tea!

So houses Nos. 3, 4, and 5 are red, white, and green. Because milk is drunk in the middle one, the Englishman drinks it. Which means the Japanese drinks coffee, and that means the Spaniard drinks juice. Because coffee is drunk in the green house, the Japanese lives there. Which means the Spaniard lives in the white house, and that means the Ukrainian lives in the blue house. Because the man who lives next door to the antique collector owns the horse, he's the Ukrainian. Which means the Englishman owns the snails. Because the man who drinks juice gardens, the Spaniard is the gardener. And finally, because the man who sings lives next door to the man with the fox, the Norwegian must own the fox, the Ukrainian must sing, the Englishman must collect stamps, and *the Japanese must own the zebra.* Good heavens! I've missed lunch!

Dear Marilyn:

As a faculty member at Bellevue Community College, I received this thinking problem: You have twelve balls that appear identical, except that one is slightly heavier or lighter than the others; using only a balance scale and three weighings, can you discover which is the "odd ball" and whether it's lighter or heavier? It's driving me nuts! Can you solve it?

Suzanne Marks
Issaquah, Washington

Here's a *super* problem for all the math classes to work through. For the first weighing, put two groups of four balls in each pan of the scale. Set the remaining four aside. If the scale balances, continue with the following heading entitled "If the First Weighing Balances." If it doesn't, skip directly to the heading entitled "If the First Weighing *Doesn't* Balance."

If the First Weighing Balances

If the first weighing balances, you know all of those eight balls are normal. For the second weighing, leave just three of these normal balls on one side of the scale, put the other five normal balls away, and put three unknown balls (from the four you set aside) on the other side of the scale. If it balances again, read (1) below. If it doesn't balance, read (2).

(1) THE SECOND WEIGHING BALANCES. Now you know the last unknown ball (from the original four you set aside) is the odd

ball. For the third weighing, leave just one normal ball on one side of the scale, take the additional five normal balls off the scale and put them away, and put the last unweighed odd ball on the other side. It will either rise or fall, telling you whether it's light or heavy. That's the answer for this sequence.

(2) THE SECOND WEIGHING DOESN'T BALANCE. But now you know whether the odd ball is light or heavy because the group (on the scale) where it's hidden either rose (if it's light) or fell (if it's heavy). For the third weighing, first put away all the normal balls, then take that "odd group" of three already on the scale and separate them all, putting one on each side of the scale and leaving one aside.

Maybe the scale will balance again. If it does, you'll know that the last ball you set aside is the odd ball, and because you already know whether it's light or heavy, that's the answer for this sequence of events.

Or maybe the scale will tilt. If it does, this will show you which is the odd ball because you already know that it's either light or heavy. If it's light, the odd ball is the one that rises, and if it's heavy, the odd ball is the one that falls. And that's the answer for this sequence of events.

If the First Weighing Doesn't Balance

Now things are going to get a little more complicated to describe, so let's number the balls. Nos. 1, 2, 3, and 4 will be the ones on the lower side of the scale, and Nos. 5, 6, 7, and 8 will be the ones on the higher side. The odd ball must be among these eight. Nos. 9, 10, 11, and 12 will be the ones that have been set aside, so these four must all be normal. That much we know.

For the second weighing, leave No. 1 on the same side (previously lower) of the scale and put Nos. 2, 3, and 4 aside. Instead of those three, substitute Nos. 6, 7, and 8 (three of the ones that were previously on the higher side of the scale). Leave No. 5 on the same side of the scale (previously higher), but add three normal balls (from the original group of four you set aside; we won't need the last normal one anymore). At this point, you have Nos. 1, 6, 7, and 8 on what was previously the lower side, and you have Nos. 5, 9, 10, and 11 on what was previously the higher side. No. 12 can be tossed into the closet.

The scale must now do one of three things: it will balance, it will tip in the opposite direction as it did before, or it will tip in the same direction it did before.

(3) THE SECOND WEIGHING BALANCES. Now you know that Nos. 2, 3, and 4 (newly set aside) contain a heavy odd ball. Why? Because when they were on the scale in the first weighing, they pulled it down against others now proven to be normal. For the third weighing, put away all the normal balls, then take that odd group of three currently set aside and separate them all, putting one on each side of the scale and leaving one aside again.

Maybe the scale will balance again. If it does, you'll know that the last ball you set aside is the odd ball, and because you already know it's heavy, that's the answer for this sequence.

Or maybe the scale will tilt. If it does, this will show you which is the odd ball because you already know that it's heavy. And that's the answer for this sequence of events.

(4) THE SECOND WEIGHING TIPS IN THE OPPOSITE DIRECTION. Now you know that Nos. 6, 7, and 8 (which changed positions on the scale) contain a light odd ball. Why? Because Nos. 1 and 5 didn't change positions, and the others on the scale are known to be normal. For the third weighing, put away all the normal balls, then take that odd group of three currently on the scale and separate them all, putting one on each side of the scale and leaving one aside.

Maybe the scale will balance again. If it does, you'll know that the last ball you set aside is the odd ball, and because you already know that it's light, that's the answer for this sequence of events.

Or maybe the scale will tilt. If it does, this will show you which is the odd ball because you already know that it's light. And that's the answer for this sequence of events.

(5) THE SECOND WEIGHING TIPS IN THE SAME DIRECTION. Now you know that No. 1 or No. 5 is the odd ball. Why? Because they're the only ones on the scale that didn't change position. If the odd ball were among Nos. 6, 7, and 8, the scale would have reversed, and the others on the scale are known to be normal. In addition, you know that either No. 1 is heavy or No. 5 is light because that's the direction the scale tips.

For the third weighing, clear everything from the scale. Then put one normal ball on one side and No. 1 on the other.

Maybe the scale will balance again. If it does, you'll know that No. 5 is the odd ball and because you already know that it's light, that's the answer for this sequence of events.

Or maybe the scale will tilt downward toward No. 1. If it does, you'll know that No. 1 is the odd ball and because you already know that it's heavy, that's the answer for this sequence.

You probably just didn't have enough paper handy!

Dear Marilyn:

My mother was dropping one hundred Hershey's Kisses into our family's five holiday stockings, one at a time from left to right, when Santa arrived and interrupted her. Later, she couldn't remember into which stocking she had last placed a Kiss. How could she continue without counting the Kisses in each stocking and without starting over, to give us all an equal number of Kisses?

Barney Bissinger
Hershey Foods
Hershey, Pennsylvania

With the remainder of the Kisses, she just reverses the direction and starts from the stocking on the right. Try it!

Answer to question on page 164: Kitty was guilty.

Fifteen

On Mysticism

"We can all have opinions about flavors, colors, and sounds, but we shouldn't have opinions about the Tooth Fairy."

Dear Marilyn:

I am deeply troubled about this and would really like to know your opinion. What do you think of Nostradamus's prediction that the world will end in 1999? I've heard all his other historical predictions have come true.

Antoinette Pierce
Inver Grove Heights, Minnesota

I wouldn't buy a harp just yet, if I were you. This physician-turned-astrologer was clearly worthy of praise for his treatment of plague victims, but his writings have worried people unnecessarily for centuries. Surely anyone who makes 1,000 prophecies (as he did) would find some of them eventually "come true," especially if people can wait for hundreds of years and find specific meaning in ambiguous, mysterious, and sometimes even utterly incomprehensible language. Some of his predictions can be readily linked with real occurrences, but others were just plain wrong. Nostradamus was surely an intelligent, foresighted man, but predicting that "all Hell will break loose" in July of 1999 doesn't mean anything, as far as I'm concerned. Why, just watch the evening news—that happens all the time.

Dear Marilyn:

A group of my friends were talking about birthdays, and one said everyone should know the day of the week, the month, and the year they were born, because it's very important in telling your future. Is there a way to find that out, even if we had to go back, say, fifty years?

Ed McCormack
Baldwin, New York

Of course, you could start with today's day and date and write it all out backward, but that would be laborious, so to save time, you can consult a "perpetual calendar," the same thing in condensed form. There are only fourteen different possible day/date configurations—one each for January 1 falling on the seven days of the week in normal years, and another each for leap years. A perpetual calendar includes all fourteen, plus a list of years. You just locate the year in question, and you'll be referred to which calendar to use.

But I can't stop there. Please understand that this information might satisfy curiosity or even be valuable for historical understanding, but it can't be used in any fashion to tell the future.

Dear Marilyn:

I always read your column, which I usually enjoy, but sometimes I get annoyed by your persistent and closed-minded opinion that superstition is all hogwash. For example, you told one reader not to continue a threatening chain letter. But I see no harm in continuing the chain letter, just in case. How do *you* know there isn't a superior force involved? Even though each and every person is entitled to his or her own opinion, I would appreciate it if you don't treat yours as fact. Loosen up!

Laura Henson
Timonium, Maryland

Real life can be difficult enough to understand; adding superstition makes it impossible. That's because superstitions are irrational beliefs that arise in people who are unaware of the laws of nature. I discourage these beliefs whenever I can because I see myself as an educator and I have compassion for people who are intellectually passive, especially about matters of fact. Such submissiveness makes them prey to every screwball with a typewriter or a megaphone, and I'm not going to stand by and watch it happen. Stand up to those crackpots, Laura! We can all have opinions about flavors, colors, and sounds, but we shouldn't have opinions about the Tooth Fairy.

Dear Marilyn:

Why isn't more serious research on ESP being done? Is it because the scientific community believes that it's pure hokum?

Marv Bensend
Atkins, Iowa

I certainly hope so.

Dear Marilyn:

I'm often at odds with people who believe in fortune-telling. What is your opinion on this subject?

Pat Cioffi
Westbury, New York

Opinion?! It's damaging to our intellectual abilities to believe too many things are matters of opinion, and this is one of them. But if you insist, my opinion is that fortune-telling is a lot of nonsense. Also in my opinion is that $1 + 1 = 2$.

Dear Marilyn:

Is there any truth in palmistry? I have a short lifeline, and I'm fearful. Were there any people in history with short lifelines but long-lived? If I knew there were, it would really put my mind at ease. Should I really be concerned?

R.D.
San Diego, California

I'm not going to reassure you with historical facts because I want you to be reassured by the truth about palmistry instead. It's entirely fictional. Those so-called "lifelines" are just ordinary creases, and the only reason a palm-reader pretends to find something of interest in your palm is so that you'll later put something of interest in *hers*.

Dear Marilyn:

Do you think the abilities of channelers are real?

Helen Thompson
Coventry, Connecticut

Only their ability to deceive innocent people is real. "Channeling" is an act staged by people who pretend to be able to "channel" the spirit of an ancient or mystical figure through themselves; they then speak words that are designed to make people think the imaginary figure is speaking, instead. I can tell you without reservation that it's all a lot of hooey.

Dear Marilyn:

One controversy that will probably never go away concerns UFOs. On one hand, you have a small number of people who each year claim to have seen them. Some of these folks say they have even taken rides on spaceships. On the other hand, you have millions of people who, skeptical by nature, wouldn't believe these stories unless a little green guy walked up and bonked them over the head with a ray gun. What would you say the chances are that our planet is actually infested with aliens?

Dave Morin
Wolcott, Connecticut

Virtually zero. Intelligent beings from outer space living here on Earth for years? Forget about it. No intelligent being would stay that long.

Dear Marilyn:

I don't want to be a wet blanket, but don't you think that it's time we did away with Halloween? It's based in witchcraft, and these days it isn't safe for kids to go door to door asking for "trick or treat" or even answering the door. I might also mention that people make themselves look pretty ridiculous, too. So why don't we remove this holiday from our calendars for good? I can assure you that it would not be missed at all.

Jeffrey Davidson
Lake Worth, Florida

"Halloween" means "Hallows' Eve" and is so called because it precedes the day known in medieval England as "All Hallows." Better known here as "All Saints' Day," November 1 is the date on which Roman Catholics and Anglicans glorify God for his saints. Before that, it marked a festival that dates back to ancient times, and because of that long history, it arrives with plenty of customs derived from beliefs that seem strange today—like ghosts roaming the Earth and witches convening to do evil deeds. But you can be grateful that at least *some* things have changed—people in England used to carve jack-o'-lanterns out of beets, potatoes, and turnips. As far as not missing the holiday is concerned, you might be right, at least for me. After all, I live in Manhattan, and depending on the neighborhood, some days it's hard to tell when it's Halloween and when it's not.

Dear Marilyn:
  Are you totally free of fear and superstition?

                                        Bill Carter
                                        Richardson, Texas

I'm not free of fear, which I think is impossible for any rational human being, but I have no superstition at all.

Sixteen

On the Arts

———

"This is art?"

Dear Marilyn:

I've got a little extra money in the bank right now, and after hearing so much about how funding for the arts is disappearing, I'm thinking about donating it. Which of them would you recommend? $1,000 means a lot to me, and I want to do the right thing.

Gina Topaz
New York, New York

Here's what I've done myself. Instead of donating your $1,000 to one group, give $100 (or whatever it takes to earn a few special privileges, like a backstage tour or attending a dress rehearsal) to ten of them. Then take advantage of whatever they offer; this is a delightful way to meet new people and to learn more about the philharmonic and the ballet and the opera and others, too. And the next time you have some extra money in the bank, you'll probably know exactly what you'd like to do with it. (But do your recipients another favor, as well. Decline to accept any free gifts, such as mugs or T-shirts or recordings. It helps their dollars stretch further.)

Dear Marilyn:

Is there a reason I get goose bumps when listening to classical music? This always happens to me, in addition to a sensation of an inner self flying.

Cathy Sarvash
Mustang, Oklahoma

You're not alone. The chief of psychiatry at Santa Maria Nuova Hospital in Florence, Italy, has even written a book about the phenomenon of soaring emotional reactions to great works of art. Not surprisingly, considering the visual magnificence of Florence, she herself has treated dozens of tourists who have been literally overwhelmed by seeing the sights. With some folks, it may go a bit too far, but the rest of us can just relax and enjoy the experience.

Dear Marilyn:

I have always thought that music is mathematical, so—disregarding arrangements and interpretations, etc., and sticking only to all the possible combinations of notes—at some point every song will have been written. No more new ones. What do you think? Please answer so I can stop thinking about it.

Cal Hawthorne
Glen Allen, Virginia

All those factors you're disregarding are what make musical variety seemingly infinite! But if we adhere to your conditions and simply strike one piano note after another in varying combinations, we'd eventually run out of songs (assuming we have a time limit for them). And if there were a finite number of words, at some point every sentence (of reasonable length) will have been written. The reason none of this should matter to you is that although there's a limit to the number of combinations of many things, there's an even stricter limit to the number of hours in your day. Just as you would never have the time to see all the paintings that have *already* been painted—let alone all the ones that *will* be painted—you don't have the time to experience all of anything else, either. Why, even if you started the day you were born, you wouldn't have the time to sample every restaurant in the world! (But I, for one, intend to at least *try*.)

Dear Marilyn:

Who, in your opinion, are the greatest male and female poets of this century?

Michael Schmidt
Greendale, Wisconsin

I think it's important for the future of our country that we, as citizens and voters, not have an opinion about everything, especially areas in which we are truly uninformed. In my case, poetry is one of those areas. According to my philosophy, then, I don't have a worthwhile opinion about this matter.

Dear Marilyn:

I find most movies boring and feel that they're not worth the time and money. Do you agree?

Gerald Cooper
Providence, North Carolina

I think they're very often well worth the money—it's astonishing that we can see a multimillion-dollar spectacle for under $10—although, depending on our financial circumstances, it might not be wise to actually spend it. But I think they're far less often worth our time, which is infinitely more valuable than our money.

Dear Marilyn:

Do you think Andy Warhol's work *100 Cans* should be considered as art?

Shawn Vermette
Springfield, Massachusetts

Yes, what else would you call oil on canvas? A science? Then again, you might simply call certain cases of oil on canvas a mess, depending on whether you'd just spilled something or it looks like that's what the artist did. But *100 Cans* doesn't look like a mess; it looks like 100 cans of Campbell's Beef Noodle soup. And the reason this doesn't look like art is that artwork has always been a combination of intellectual craft and social statement, with the eloquence of the former overwhelmingly dominating the latter, at least in the past. In modern times, though, the element of craft has diminished while the element of statement has grown, and Andy Warhol's work is a good example of that. Devoid of intellect, its content is entirely social. But it's still art.

Dear Marilyn:

On a recent trip, I had an opportunity to visit a museum of modern art. One of the more striking, albeit obscure, pieces was a work that consisted of a large canoe-like structure made out of metal and glass on the floor, a stuffed alligator hanging on the wall behind it, and hanging next to the alligator, the following series of numbers, in bright neon:

1, 1, 2, 3, 5, 8, 13, 21, 34, 55, 89, 144, 233, 377, 610, 987

I couldn't figure this thing out for the life of me. Can you? Does it mean anything? Or is the artist pulling a fast one on all of us?

Gary Tucker
Seattle, Washington

I think the artist is pulling a fast one, all right, but not because of the numbers, which are known as a Fibonacci series. More correctly beginning with 0, each number is the sum of the previous two numbers. This is art?

Dear Marilyn:

Which American artist from this century will be the most revered in 500 years?

Brian Hendrick
New Port Richey, Florida

I think it's going to be Norman Rockwell. I don't believe that the average American 500 years from now will pay serious attention to canvasses that appear to have had paint spilled on them. (And I don't think the average American today pays serious attention, either.) Think of what a treasure it would be to find—today—the works of an eighteenth-century artist who specialized in richly detailed, affectionately anecdotal observances of everyday life in the small towns of early America—especially if most other eighteenth-century works consisted of subjects like randomly-placed brush strokes and people with three eyes. Remember—there are no Michelangelos or Leonardos around these days. Who would be Rockwell's competition?

Dear Marilyn:

Apparently the understanding of the meaning of Picasso's art requires a more developed mind than I have. When I once asked an artist what his own painting—which consisted of two splotches and three lines—meant, he replied, "If you don't know, then I can't tell you." You're eloquent; would you please give me an idea of what to look for or try to feel when I view a Picasso?

Anonymous
Franklin, Indiana

For the answer, let me quote Pablo Picasso himself, who stated the secret of his success very succinctly. "I'm a joker who has understood his epoch and has extracted all he possibly could from the stupidity, greed, and vanity of his contemporaries." It's difficult to be more eloquent than that.

Dear Marilyn:

Fie upon thee, Lady Marilyn! Picasso did *not* say what you said he did in an earlier column. That alleged confession was concocted by the unscrupulous Giovanni Papini in 1951. It was cynical of you to accept Papini's blast without question. A retraction is in order.

Joseph Bolt, Ph.D.
Professor of Art History Emeritus
University of Alabama
Tuscaloosa, Alabama

I blew it on this one. Your letter had the ring of truth, so we checked into it carefully, even going so far as to obtain a copy of Giovanni Papini's book called *The Black Book* in its original Italian. But Papini was not unscrupulous. His work is simply a satire that contains imaginary interviews with numerous famous characters—a work of fiction that was widely misinterpreted as fact throughout Europe and the United States, as well. The mistaken "quotes" have been repeated to this day, and I hope this column will help to bring a halt to them.

So, dear readers, Picasso did *not* say, "I'm a joker who has understood his epoch and has extracted all he possibly could from the stupidity, greed, and vanity of his contemporaries."

But he *should* have!

Seventeen

On the Personal Side

"I practice what I preach.
That's why I try <u>never</u> to preach."

Dear Marilyn:

How do you manage to relate to your readers? I know you must have come from a fancy family and had every advantage while you were growing up, too.

Edna Mortie
San Diego, California

Forget the "fancy family" stuff, Edna. Both my grandfathers were coal miners from the "old country." Grandpa vos Savant died in the mines while helping a friend survive a disaster there, and Grandpa Mach was crippled in a mining accident.

And as far as advantages are concerned, my father worked long hours while I was growing up, my mother insisted on impossibly high standards of behavior, and my two older brothers showed me all sorts of things that young ladies weren't supposed to know anything about. So yes, I guess I *did* have every advantage!

Dear Marilyn:

What is your earliest memory of yourself or your family?

Ondrea Fletcher
Chesterfield, Virginia

I'm not really sure. There are many fragmentary ones—for example, I remember things like an overstuffed chair with doilies, and my brothers "watching" a big radio, and my mother wearing a flowered dress with an apron over it, and my father tapping his hat at a little angle, and an old man down the street with a sackful of pigeons—but none of those memories included a calendar.

Dear Marilyn:

We desperately want to have a letter published in your column. It's sort of our dream. Therefore, we decided to batch a whole heap of questions together so that you would be more likely to print one. Please realize how incredibly desperate we are, and if nothing else, take pity on us. (Question No. 12) What were you like as a child?

Justin Lee and Chaim Karczag
West Orange, New Jersey

I was thin, nervous, athletic, and I never shut up. (Don't complain, fellas. Question No. 12 was a heck of a lot better than the one about an infinite number of people boarding a bus with an infinite number of seats.)

Dear Marilyn:

I have been impressed by the clarity of your explanations about why you took your mother's maiden name, and I'd like to ask you a further question about the unconventional step you took. Did your parents bring you up to question authority?

Tabatha Yeatts
Iowa City, Iowa

No. My parents brought me up to be so unquestioning of authority that I seldom questioned even their own authority with matters of any substance. In a way, this seems inhibiting; but in another way, it makes sense. Children aren't mature enough to question authority in a constructive way, and my parents didn't want a young radical in the house. It wasn't until I was in my twenties that I began to realize that authorities can have poor ideas, but at least I was old enough by then to know that it's the idea that should be questioned—not the authority.

Dear Marilyn:

What inspires your curiosity most?

Brindo Vas
Lanai City, Hawaii

Why, it's people, of course. That's one of the main reasons I write this column. Through their letters, I'm in direct contact with a changing stream of tens of thousands of Americans, and it's been a unique learning experience. Over the years, I've gained firsthand knowledge of what folks know and what they don't know, including the "what, where, when, why, and how" of American thinking. What could be more fascinating?

Dear Marilyn:
   What do you think is your very best quality?

                                             Ray Kempe
                                             Belleville, Illinois

My best quality is that I know what my weaknesses are.

Dear Marilyn:
   Do you always practice what you preach?

                                             David Marmonet
                                             Evansville, Indiana

Yes. That's why I try *never* to preach.

Dear Marilyn:
   Which woman (or women) do you admire the most?

                                             Jonelle Hudson
                                             Upland, California

Let me start by telling you about the *other* ones. I don't admire women who become famous, wealthy, or powerful because of their husbands. And if those wives embrace the spotlight themselves, they become harmful examples for womankind, especially if they believe that they're *good* examples. I also don't admire women who obtained important positions because they're female, unless that played as minor a role as it used to play for men.

   Whom does that leave? It leaves a small but growing group of strong, independent women whose contributions to society are outstanding and who achieved prominence entirely for that reason. I admire them all.

Dear Marilyn:
   You probably intimidate most men. Have you ever played dumb in order to make a man feel more comfortable? Or do you just behave normally and think, "To heck with them"?

                                             Andrea Harding
                                             Pasco, Washington

You didn't give me enough choices—I behave normally in order to make men feel more comfortable, and I think the stereotype of men having such fragile self-images that they want women to act dumb around them is a lot of hooey. For example, envision Marilyn Monroe "as is." Now envision Marilyn Monroe with Meryl Streep's intelligence, instead. Which one would more men want?

Dear Marilyn:
    How has writing a national column changed your life?
                                            Steve Jarrell
                                            Hanahan, South Carolina

Writing a national column has educated me, confounded me, amused me, inspired me, enlightened me, and absorbed way more time than I thought it would.

On the plus side, I now have a grasp of both how and what Americans think. From personally reading tens of thousands of letters every year (speed-reading, that is!), I know much of what people understand and what they don't understand; what will rouse them to action and what will bore them to sleep; what they worry about and what they take for granted (often at their peril). This added perspective has made me both more political (publicly) and more philosophical (privately).

On the minus side, I've had a substantial loss of privacy, but maybe it's a blessing in disguise. I'm now on my best behavior 99 percent of the time instead of 90 percent, like before. (Then again, that 10 percent was often the most fun.)

Dear Marilyn:
    I mailed you a simple question about five months ago. While I didn't think that the question was of sufficient interest perhaps to be published in your column, I took for granted that you would have the courtesy of replying to me. Remarkably and much to my surprise, I have not heard from you. Why, since you are so very smart, do you not think it would be the smart thing to answer all correspondence re-

ceived? Your not doing it is, quite frankly, somewhat of a disappointment.

Gerardo Joffe
San Francisco, California

I don't reply to all my mail because I don't want to send my readers
form letters, and I don't have enough waking hours to write them myself. If I receive a minimum of 500 letters a week (and sometimes it's
much more), and I take only fifteen minutes to read and reply to each
one, that's 7,500 minutes, or 125 hours a week. If I sleep only 6 hours
a night, that means I have only 126 waking hours in which to do this.
So I suppose I can. But I'm sure going to have to eat fast.

(And no, there's no simple method of determining whether a long
number is divisible by 7.)

Dear Marilyn:
I haven't written to you before, but my friend has. He says he's sent
you three questions, but he's never seen any of them appear in your
column. Can you give us an idea of what type of question probably
won't appear?

Michael McGee
Chicago, Illinois

I'd rather not do that. Any and all questions are welcome—narrow and
broad, superficial and deep. I want my readers to write with what interests them and not restrict themselves in any way. Little issues can
have big appeal, and big issues can be addressed in a small amount of
space. And every letter has an impact on me personally, regardless of
whether it gets published, and that, in turn, has an impact on what I
write in the future. I learn how people think, what they feel, and why
they do the things they do.
Even the fellow who wrote to me with the following question is ap-
preciated: "Do you know of an algorithm for determining how to slice
any kind of rectangular parallelepiped with integral sides into unit
cubes using the minimum number of planar cuts if you allow re-
arrangement of the pieces between the cuts?" The answer is "yes," but

I'm not going to take the space to explain because I feel confident of only one person in the world interested in the reply—him!

Dear Marilyn:
    Can you answer every question without a book, or do you go talk to people, or what? P.S. I'm nine. P.P.S. Please tell the truth.

                                        Michelle Ciapanna
                                        Liverpool, Pennsylvania

I answer most questions myself, *but* I never stop talking to people and I never stop reading books. That's how we all learn, dear, and I'm not an exception. For example, how would I even have known the results of the last presidential election without having seen it on television, heard about it on the radio or from another person, or read about it in a newspaper or magazine?
    Moreover, our civilization is as advanced as it is today mainly because our ancestors learned to write down what they knew and pass it on from generation to generation, making more and more progress with each passing year. So if I can answer a question about a light bulb, you can thank Thomas Edison for it.

Dear Marilyn:
    How large is your research staff?

                                        Scott Mayo
                                        Mobile, Alabama

What research staff? My "staff" for this column consists of a single downtrodden but cheerful individual who is overworked and under-paid and who handles everything from answering the telephone to typing at the speed of light (with two fingers, yet) to racing around the city doing oddball jobs like verifying an original foreign quotation from 1951, locating just the right color flowers for the photographer in my office, and retrieving me from some distant location when I can't find a cab in the rain. (With a research staff, I could write a whole magazine.)

Dear Marilyn:

Do you ever feel unjustly criticized? I know I can't always be right, but when I'm right, I will argue the point.

Vivian Renetta Gifford
Fort Worth, Texas

Yes, but I don't have your ability to argue the point. For example, nearly every time I answer a math or science question (or any kind of tricky question with a black-and-white answer), some readers will write and insist that I was wrong. Of course, if I'm wrong, I will say so in print. But I can't defend each correct answer or the column would be filled with explanations every week. (I take the space to explain only when the number of protestors is massive.) And when I don't comment in print, these people then write back and say I'm afraid to admit to an error!

Dear Marilyn:

How do you handle people who will criticize you no matter what you do?

Gary Agron
Sedalia, Missouri

I listen to them. That's what they want the most, it won't do any harm just to listen, and who knows?—they may be right, in which case I'll have a chance to improve myself.

Dear Marilyn:

If someone hit you, would you hit back?

Megan Wood
Lancaster, Pennsylvania

No, I'm not that easily provoked to action. There may be a time to hit, but that may not be the time.

Dear Marilyn:

I've been reading quite a few articles about you lately, and I was wondering, how do *you* feel when you read them? That is, how do you feel when you read an article about yourself?

Rondie Howard
Sterling, Illinois

Reading an article about yourself often feels like getting a bad haircut. Yes, it's still your hair, and yes, it's still your head, but it's not the way you usually present yourself to the world!

Dear Marilyn:

As "vos Savant" is your mother's name, and your father's name was "Mach," is it possible that you are related to the famous physicist-philosopher Ernst Mach (1838–1916), who also strongly influenced Einstein?

Ernest Parent
Hyattsville, Maryland

This is what I've been told, and although the name is uncommon and my father's relatives do come from the same part of Europe, I've never taken the trouble to find out. (Most people know the name from the term "Mach number," which relates the velocity of an object to the velocity of sound, but Mach is familiar to scientists and philosophers for more important concepts. His inertial theories were cited by Einstein as one of the inspirations for the theories of relativity, and Mach's writings helped to generate the school of philosophy known as logical positivism.)

Besides, I think I should quit while I'm ahead. Although searching one's genealogy can be an exciting experience, it seems that for every one poet in your family tree, you find half a dozen pirates.

Dear Marilyn:

If scientists of the future, as portrayed in *Jurassic Park,* may someday replicate life from DNA preserved in ancient resin, why couldn't *you* give a volunteer mosquito a taste and then dunk the critter into resin, label it, and leave your DNA to science? Better you than some old dinosaur!

Gordon Greb
Chico, California

Hmmm. I hope that's a compliment. Regardless, I've decided to leave some money to scientific research, which I think they'll appreciate far more than a dead mosquito. But thanks, anyway. I'm glad to know that you think I'm more desirable to have around than an ugly carnivorous reptile the size of a bus.

Dear Marilyn:

Do you mind if I name a calf after you? "Marilyn" is one of the smarter animals to be born on our farm. Also, I am proud that she is the first heifer born of my newly acquired artificial-insemination skills. I thought it appropriate to name her after someone I admire.

Karen Morrison
Smithville, Ohio

Mind?! Why, I'm honored! But I sure hope "Marilyn" is a dairy cow. I don't want to have to worry every time I look down at a plate of roast beef.

Eighteen

On the Funniest Questions

Marilyn, how do they fit all that
hot air into blow-dryers?
Why don't they ever run out?

You know, there are some questions that need no answer—like *these*!

✖

Dear Marilyn:

As a sufferer of menopausal "hot flashes," I have experienced the ability of the human body to comfortably withstand freezing temperatures without the aid of warm clothing or external heat. Has science ever attempted to study this phenomenon with an eye toward eliminating our dependence on Middle East oil? Think of the savings if we could scrap the need for central heating!

> L.F.
> Oakland City, Indiana

✖

Dear Marilyn:

Why does a pickle become luminescent when 110 volts of alternating current pass through it?

> B.J. and D.K.
> Yosemite, California

✖

Dear Marilyn:
Why are bananas crooked?

> K.S.
> Glen Burnie, Maryland

✖

Dear Marilyn:
Did dinosaurs eat corn?

> J.R.
> Vienna, Ohio

✖

Dear Marilyn:

Is there a difference between Rocky Road ice cream and Heavenly Hash ice cream? I say no!

> J.S.
> Greenville, South Carolina

✖

Dear Marilyn:

  Why are chicken fingers called chicken fingers if chickens don't
have fingers?

S.M.
Scotch Plains, New Jersey

✖

Dear Marilyn:

  Why has no one ever thought of milking his or her pet dogs or cats?

E.H.
Great Falls, Virginia

✖

Dear Marilyn:

  Can you poison a hog? Supposedly, they don't have veins.

B.C.
Parchman, Mississippi

✖

Dear Marilyn:

  Do bats have noses?

E.S.W.
Huntsville, Alabama

✖

Dear Marilyn:

  Do turtles ever get high blood pressure?

J.H.
Carteret, New Jersey

✖

Dear Marilyn:

Do worms ever die?

C.J.
Toledo, Ohio

Dear Marilyn:

If one were to tie a snake into a loose square knot, would the snake be able to untie itself?

A.J.
Knoxville, Tennessee

Dear Marilyn:

Do oysters get bored? How can you tell?

J.H.
Carteret, New Jersey

Dear Marilyn:

Why do dragonflies like to hang out on car antennas?

C.S.
Charleston, South Carolina

Dear Marilyn:

Was God asleep when he invented mosquitoes? If not, what is their purpose? You know everything, don't disappoint me.

M.T.
St. Peter, Minnesota

Dear Marilyn:

Why does a wool sweater shrink when washed? The same wool doesn't shrink on sheep when they stand in the rain.

J.C.A.
Las Vegas, Nevada

✕

Dear Marilyn:

How come Mickey the Mouse is taller than his dog Pluto?

C.D.
Olney, Maryland

✕

Dear Marilyn:

Would you please set the facts straight for me. Is Elvis really dead or is he still alive?

J.H.
Gretna, Nebraska

✕

Dear Marilyn:

How many miles do you estimate Arnold Palmer has walked in his lifetime?

B.C.
Grand Rapids, Michigan

✕

Dear Marilyn:

Can you find out if Julio Iglesias and Don Ho are brothers? Somewhere I heard that their last name is Lampone.

K.K.
Pittsburgh, Pennsylvania

✕

Dear Marilyn:

May I have the addresses of the cast of the *McGyver* series, so that I can send them each a Fashionably Personalized Initial Bookmark?

K.P.

Manchester, Georgia

Dear Marilyn:

I have a $25 bet riding on this question. Where is *Hidden Valley* and do they have cable?

T.S.

Waterford, Pennsylvania

Dear Marilyn:

Why is it that in all those old mysteries they always said, "The butler did it"? Were butlers really so terrible?

M.R.

Boynton Beach, Florida

Dear Marilyn:

Why do men feel like they have to have the remote control? All right, I'm sitting on the couch watching *Jeopardy!* and my dad comes down. I left the remote control unguarded. Bad mistake. He grabs it so fast I hardly notice. So I think it's okay, as long as he doesn't change the channel. I get to "Double Jeopardy," and I'm winning against the lawyer, Ray, and CLICK. Next thing I know I'm watching *Kung Fu: The Legend Lives.* How do you stop this?

B.H.

Frederick, Maryland

Dear Marilyn:

My friend and I know every detail about the Blues Brothers. We even know that their license-plate number is BDR529. But one thing stumps us. The car they drove is a Dodge—but what is the model?

Anonymous
Seattle, Washington

☒

Dear Marilyn:

Please settle this disagreement between my boyfriend and me. In a song popular during the 1960s, the lyrics read, "Ooh eee ooh ah ah wing wang walla walla bing bang ooh eee ooh ah ah wing wang walla walla bing bang." My boyfriend insists it is "Ooh eee ooh ah ah ching chang walla walla bing bang ooh eee ooh ah ah ching chang walla walla bing bang."

Who is correct?

S.S.
Cape Girardeau, Missouri

☒

Dear Marilyn:

Do you know the words to the Notre Dame song that starts out, "Cheer, cheer for old Notre Dame; you bring the liquor, I'll bring the dame"? It has slipped my mind, and I would love to hear it again.

M.M.
San Diego, California

☒

Dear Marilyn:

I was challenged with this riddle when I was in the sixth grade and still have not come up with a good answer. As I am now going through a divorce and discovering who I really am, I find that my life will not be complete until I know the answer. Is there a word in the English language that rhymes with "orange"? Obviously, this won't make my life complete, but it's a good start.

T.S.H.
Mesa, Arizona

Dear Marilyn:

Could you please tell me the number of shades of green? After driving and looking around at the scenery, I have decided there must be many.

P.P.
Hannibal, Missouri

Dear Marilyn:

We have all heard the expression "Once in a blue moon," but how common is it? Also, what other colors does the moon come in?

J.C.
New York, New York

Dear Marilyn:

I wonder if the Earth is at a different angle in the morning than it is at night. In the morning, I have to put something against the front door to hold it open. In the night it stays open by itself.

A.A.L.
Austin, Texas

Dear Marilyn:

While in South Carolina recently, I noticed that north is southeast of due west. How can you explain this?

E.J.F.
Lake Worth, Florida

Dear Marilyn:

I've always wanted to go to Europe, but I can't afford it. So, since the Earth rotates every 24 hours, why couldn't I shoot straight up in some sort of contraption, hover above, and let Europe come to *me*?

A.M.S.
El Dorado, Arkansas

Dear Marilyn:

If everyone on Earth walked west at the same time, would the Earth spin faster (1) during the walk? (2) after the walk? If either answer is "yes," how much shorter would the day get?

S.D.
Glendale Heights, Indiana

Dear Marilyn:

I am riding on a sailboat going 50 mph in a northerly direction. At the same time, a wind is blowing from the south at 50 mph. My question is this: Does the wind cause my ponytail to blow toward my face or away from it?

M.S.M.
Lafayette, Louisiana

Dear Marilyn:

Do we really need thunder and lightning?

C.B.
Pittsburgh, Pennsylvania

Dear Marilyn:

You never did tell me why there is no static electricity in southern Luzon, in the Philippines.

R.B.
Forestville, California

Dear Marilyn:
Do you know where I could find an antigravity machine?
J.S.
Plainfield, Indiana

Dear Marilyn:
I am a highly adventurous person who is bored with bungee-jumping, skydiving, and hang-gliding. Thus, I have decided to try flying. But I'm wondering how long I need to build my wingspan for my 122-pound 5'2" frame? How wide should my wings be? What do you suggest I make my wings out of?
T.R.
Minneapolis, Minnesota

Dear Marilyn:
If you were an airplane, what type of aircraft would you want to be?
S.A.
San Antonio, Texas

Dear Marilyn:
I've heard that people have magnetism in their noses. Is this true?
M.W.
Manlius, New York

Dear Marilyn:
Can you wiggle your ears?
T.B.
Colorado Springs, Colorado

Dear Marilyn:

After a successful heart transplant, is the patient able to recite the poems that the donor knew by heart?

J.M.S.
San Pedro, California

Dear Marilyn:

From the waist up or down, which half of the human body is the most useful to life?

P.M.
Mount View, Oklahoma

Dear Marilyn:

Why is it that all the fingers have a name (thumb, index, middle, ring, and pinky), but for toes, it's only big toe, little toe? What are the other three called? ("Piggies" don't count.)

J.D.
Augusta, Georgia

Dear Marilyn:

If you had two socks made of the exact same material except one was black and the other white, which sock would make your foot sweat more?

M.
Lewiston, Maine

Dear Marilyn:

Can you list possible places and things that could have happened to a sock from the time it was taken off the foot until it should have come out of the laundry clean?

M.H.
Fond du Lac, Wisconsin

Dear Marilyn:

If all large nations are in debt, where is all the money?

K.B.

Morse, Texas

Dear Marilyn:

When a corporation declares bankruptcy under federal statute, it does so pursuant to Chapter 11. What happened in Chapters 1–10?

R.A.F.

St. Augustine, Florida

Dear Marilyn:

Please tell me why Lincoln is pictured facing right on the penny when all the other American coins picture their presidents facing left. It really irritates me!

G.T.

Delano, Georgia

Dear Marilyn:

There must be tons of loose change lying around the houses of this country, either thrown in some container, lost in the cracks of couches, down in the seats of cars, or just generally stuck away and forgotten about. Does this affect the economy in any way?

A.F.

Russellville, Alabama

Dear Marilyn:

What's the price of a new set of *Encyclopedia Britannica*? I've been trying to find out since 1946, but all I've ever gotten are salesmen at my door.

M.E.W.

Milford, Connecticut

X

Dear Marilyn:

It appears to me that in the past hundred years, an overwhelming amount of progress has been made in the world. What did all those people do for the first two thousand years?

R.F.
Manassas, Virginia

X

Dear Marilyn:

What property of matter allows for the movement of popcorn residue inside of a plastic bowl to the outside of the plastic bowl? Also, do you think that this could one day be applied to some future form of transportation?

T.H.
Corte Madera, California

X

Dear Marilyn:

Why can't we put all the unrecyclable styrofoam in the fault lines down here to kill two birds with one stone? It wouldn't take up space in our landfills and maybe would prevent earthquakes.

S.A.
Encinitas, California

X

Dear Marilyn:

How did the town of Oxnard, California, get its name? Is there such a thing as Horsenard? Or Camelnard?

W.R.
Porterville, California

X

Dear Marilyn:

How do they make glitter? Sequins, I can understand. But glitter?

                                S.S.
                                Huntsville, Alabama

☒

Dear Marilyn:

I do not understand women. Would the study of quantum mechanics help?

                                J.B.
                                Parsippany, New Jersey

☒

Dear Marilyn:

My mother-in-law is 52 years old. Is it true that if I travel off into space at the speed of light for one year, she will be 152 years old when I return? Sounds like a good deal.

                                L.T.B.
                                Hancock, Virginia

☒

Dear Marilyn:

If M&Ms melt in your mouth and not in your hand, what about your underarm? I want to give it a test, but my mom won't let me.

                                M.C.
                                Granite City, Illinois

☒

Dear Marilyn:

I admire you for your intelligence. I'm hoping some of it will rub off on my little brother if he reads your column enough. Do you have any kids? If not, would you like to have my little brother?

                                A.B.
                                Delray Beach, Florida

✖

Dear Marilyn:
　Do you believe in God?
　Which television shows have you appeared on?

A.R.
Berkeley, California

✖

Dear Marilyn:
　I really enjoy your column. You have a great sense of humor. If the columnist thing doesn't work out, you should do stand-up comedy.

R.P.
Brentwood, Maryland

✖

Dear Marilyn:
　What percentage of the questions you receive are dumb?

Eugene Michael
Fort Pierce, Florida

Hardly any. Some just strike me as funny. For example, "Why are manhole covers round?" is a perfectly serious question, and a number of readers wrote to suggest that they're round because that keeps them from falling into the manhole. But that's beside the point. Manhole covers don't tumble into the manholes because the manholes have a lip around their edges that makes them a little smaller than the covers. Roundness doesn't keep the covers from falling in. *Lips* do. Oh, for heaven's sake. Now *I'm* the one who sounds dumb.

Do you have a question?
Send it to:

ASK MARILYN VOS SAVANT
Ansonia Station
Post Office Box 967
New York, New York 10023

Because of the volume of mail, we regret that personal replies will not be possible.

Marilyn vos Savant was born in St. Louis, Missouri, the daughter of Marina vos Savant and Joseph Mach. She is married to Robert Jarvik, M.D., the inventor of the Jarvik-7 artificial heart. They live in Manhattan. Marilyn vos Savant was listed in the *Guinness Book of World Records* for five years under "Highest IQ" for both childhood and adult scores, and she has now been inducted into the Guinness Hall of Fame. She is a writer, lecturer, and spends additional time assisting her husband in the artificial-heart program. She is a member of the Board of Directors of the National Council on Economic Education and a member of the National Advisory Board of the National Association for Gifted Children. Her special interests are politics and leadership; quality education and thinking; humanitarian medicine and research. She describes herself as an "independent" with regard to politics and religion, and only an "armchair" feminist.

Marilyn vos Savant writes the "Ask Marilyn" question-and-answer column for *Parade,* the Sunday magazine for more than 340 newspapers nationwide, with a circulation of 37 million and a readership of 81 million, the largest in the world. Past book publications include: *The Power of Logical Thinking,* published in hardcover; *More Marilyn,* published in hardcover and trade paperback; *"I've Forgotten Everything I Learned in School!",* published in hardcover and trade paperback; *The World's Most Famous Math Problem: The Proof of Fermat's Last Theorem and Other Mathematical Mysteries,* published in trade paperback; and *Ask Marilyn,* published in hardcover, trade paperback, and mass market; all by St. Martin's Press.